THE ACTOR'S
script

THE ACTOR'S
script

script analysis for performers

Charles S. Waxberg

HEINEMANN ■ Portsmouth, NH

HEINEMANN
361 Hanover Street
Portsmouth, NH 03801–3912

Offices and agents throughout the world

Library of Congress Cataloging-in-Publication Data

Waxberg, Charles S.
    The actor's script : script analysis for performers / Charles S. Waxberg.
       p.   cm.
    Includes bibliographical references.
    ISBN 0-435-07031-2 (alk. paper)
    1. Drama—Explication.   I. Title.
PN1631.W28   1997
808.2—dc21   97-40174
                                       CIP

Graphics designed by Mark A. Harmon

Editor: Lisa A. Barnett
Production: Vicki Kasabian
Cover and book design: Jenny Jensen Greenleaf
Manufacturing: Louise Richardson

Printed in the United States of America on acid-free paper
15 14 13 12   VP   13 14 15 16

To Stella Adler

And to each of my teachers,
including the students.

■

Contents

Acknowledgments

Theatre is a tradition graciously passed from one generation to the next; I cannot take credit for a single idea in this book. Its concepts are all only branches from a tree that germinated thousands of years ago. Therefore, I happily express my deepest thanks and grateful homage to those people whose lifework, teachings, and writings have contributed immeasurably. Of course the late Konstantin Stanislavsky and Stella Adler must head the list, closely followed by: David Ball, James Tripp, Alice Winston, Elisabeth Orion, Julienne Empric, Paul Kuritz, Harold Clurman, Robert Lewis, David Scanlon, Eric Bentley, Michael Pierce, Howard Stein, and a few hundred students whose questions teach more than my answers.

Introduction

You can tell very little about a stranger who's reading a book or a magazine. Perhaps you make general assumptions from the subject matter, but little else. However, if you see someone reading a play script, you inevitably think they are in theatre or taking a dramatic literature course because very few people read plays for pleasure. There is a reason for this: Plays are meant to be performed, not read. Until a script is married with the artistic contributions of actor, designer, technician, director, and—finally—audience, it is unfinished. A novel completes its circle with one reader as a painting does with one viewer. But the performing arts require collaborative contributions, and for this reason, scripts are intentionally incomplete. And since, as works of writing, they are incomplete, they are rarely read for pleasure by everyday people.

The first contact an audience has with a play is the last stage of its development. They hear about it, see an advertisement, get an invitation, receive a recommendation from friends, or encounter similar publicity. These are the final ingredients, but the genesis of that play began in the mind of a playwright. An idea came from some unidentifiable place we call inspiration and seeded the mind. All life begins with seeds, and plays are artistic re-creations of life.

The play was born with that seeded idea and evolved first into a script. Then the script was collaborated on by other artists and grew to production. Each artistic choice, technical invention, and dramatic interpretation was created to bring that idea to life in the fullest, most communicative form possible. The script is the tangible life of that seed, and everyone involved uses it as a reference just as everyone on a new building site refers to a blueprint.

But what exactly is a script? *A script is nothing less or more than a sequential listing of actions.* Actions include anything that is done, and a script lists these actions in sequence that will result in the completed work being brought to life by all the artists involved. Although it may include descriptions of location and character, this is not crucial, especially in twentieth-century works. A script is no more a play than a blueprint is a house or a recipe is a cake.

Examine the beginning of Harold Pinter's *Betrayal*. Pinter begins the play with the briefest description necessary to communicate the mise-en-scène: time and location. *"Pub. 1977. Spring. Noon."*

If *Betrayal* were a novel, he might have described in great detail the appearance and atmosphere of the pub—the stained-glass windows, the dark oak tables, the presence of music and din, or the class and demeanor of the other patrons. But Pinter acknowledges that these details are design and directorial interpretations and the audience will *see* them. A playwright chooses as few words as possible to convey an idea. (Playwrights such as Shaw or O'Neill went to great lengths to describe the many details of locale and character appearance, but this was when printing-press paper became plentiful and people were reading plays for pleasure. Playwrights wrote with this in mind.)

After Pinter communicates the mise en scène, the play truly begins, or, rather, the sequence of actions start:

1st action: *Emma is sitting at a corner table.* [or "Emma sits."]

2nd action: *Jerry approaches with drinks.* [Then, specifying more the nature of what he is carrying in order to illuminate character efficiently.] *A pint of bitter for him, a glass of wine for her.*

3rd action: *He sits.*

4th action: *They smile,*

5th action: *toast each other silently,*

6th action: *drink.*

7th action: *He sits back and*

8th action: *looks at her.*

There is an action in dramatic writing that is so common—so universal—that there is a shorthand for it: So-and-so *says*. This is recognized by the name centered over the dialogue or preceding it with a colon:

9th action: [Jerry says]: *Well . . .*

10th action: [Emma says]: *How are you? Etc. . . .*

Often, you will find a nonspecific action, *pause* or *beat*, which means that the playwright is giving you a period of time before the next action begins. This is not an indication to *wait*, but more of a *free space* to fill with the action that serves your character or your production best.

So, basically, a script is no different than a good recipe. (Or for that matter, a bad script—a bad recipe.) Take eggs, flour, water, yeast, and sugar (the ingredients), mix, let it rise, do this, do that (the actions), and you get bread. Take a sixteenth-century Danish castle, a prince, his uncle/stepfather, a ghost, a girlfriend, some buddies, and others (the ingredients), do this, say that, kill them (the actions), and you get *Hamlet*. A script is no less or more a sequential listing of actions and ingredients than a blueprint, a dress pattern, a computer program, DNA, travel directions, dance steps, or any instruction manual.

However, some instruction manuals are easier than others. One could wager that no one reads the directions on a tube of toothpaste except for those die-hards who must read something—anything— while in the bathroom. Who listens to the "how to fasten seat belts" directions on an airplane? You might peruse the instructions to a new microwave oven only for details that explain its features. The manuals that come with a new VCR are studied and, hopefully, understood.

Items and processes that are more complex have more complex instruction manuals. And complex instruction manuals are more difficult to understand.

Plays are about the human condition. They use human behavior to demonstrate a unique view of this human condition. And there is arguably nothing more complex than our species and its societies. A play attempts to present one facet—one illuminating insight—of the world in which people live and have lived. And to re-create life, even one facet of it, is an extremely intricate and subtle task. The script is the manual—the play's DNA—to re-create this life. It cannot merely be read like a book—*it must be studied*. Its actions are deliberately unspecific. Exactly *how* does Emma ask, "How are you?" How *long* does she sit before Jerry enters? What are they *doing* during the *pause*? Even with the elaborate descriptions of Shaw or the specific stage directions of Arthur Miller, the latitude— and necessity—for interpretation is enormous.

The more actors know about *all* script elements, the better their choices. The actor who understands play structure will be able to build the most powerful climax and create thematic completion. The actor who understands psychological motivation will best create believable, stirring characters. The actor who understands the playwright's process will best be able to fulfill those ideas and inherent theatricality. The more versed actors are in reading scripts, the more adroit they will be at making strong, powerful choices that illuminate the play and entrance an audience.

This book examines the most universal elements in scripts so that actors can intelligently interpret and use them. When you finish reading here, you will be able to pick up *any* script and pull the most useful elements, enliven the largest statements, and recognize the playwright's subtle signposts that point the way to strong theatrical conflict and rich performance.

1 The Framework

Before Thespis in the fifth century B.C. supposedly put a mask in front of his face and "became" another person, writing existed to be read. The closest thing to dramatic writing was epic poetry recited aloud. But when the *enactment* replaced or accompanied the narration, a new style of writing—drama—began.

As any new technique evolves, practitioners explore its expanses and limitations with success and failure. Like today, much of what was written was brilliant and much was garbage. Our present civilization has only a small percentage of the brilliant works extant—who saves garbage?

Two hundred years after Thespis presumably lived, the Athenian philosopher and critic Aristotle studied all the dramatic brilliance and garbage. Eventually, he outlined his discoveries for effective dramatic writing (as well as other forms) in *The Poetics*. He examined how the audience's heart was captured, when their minds were reached, and what involved them most. With our omnipresent entertainment in television and film, it's hard to imagine that acting out an exciting story was ever a new idea, but reading *The Poetics* reveals the thrill of Aristotle's energy and excitement as he molded observation into technique. (Read it; it's the first book ever written on script analysis.)

It's equally important to know that these plays were written and produced by men, and for a predominantly male audience. Apart from the obvious anatomical differences, there are chemical and character distinctions to the sexes. Certainly there are individual exceptions—and also there are present in each sex many facets of the opposite—but *generally* there are approaches that men relate to more often than woman, and others that woman connect with more often than men. For the past two millennia, the styles of dramatic writing evolved to provoke masculine interest. Only in this century has a feminine approach to playwriting powerfully emerged, redefining the structure of effective drama. Both styles will be explained in this chapter.

First, one thing must be clearly defined: *masculine* does not mean *male* and *feminine* does not mean *female*. Nor do these structures imply that male playwrights write linear, masculine scripts, and female playwrights write circular, feminine scripts. In fact, very rarely will you find a play that is rigidly one structure or the other, almost as rarely as you will find a human being who is unwaveringly feminine or masculine.

But you will find most people (and living things, for that matter) predominate one or the other at any point in time, regardless of gender. Scripts, the living things of the stage, are created with an overall vision that is generally masculine or feminine. Yet, like people, every script will most likely have elements of both, and, like people, they can be categorized as fundamentally masculine or feminine.

The vast majority of plays, film, and television produced in the world base their dramatic structure around Aristotle's masculine framework; Western civilization has accustomed itself to this effective storytelling architecture. What follows is a cutaway blueprint of this infrastructure.

Part I: The Masculine (Aristotelian) Script

Plot: Aristotle's Unity of Action

In *Tropic of Cancer*, Henry Miller defined art as the creation of order out of chaos. Life is chaotic: Innocent children are murdered, corrupt politicians go unpunished, creative people die young from some unstoppable virus. Faith may give us the peace to believe that there is an unfathomable justice in the world, but we ourselves too often cannot see it. Art creates order just as faith allows our mind to accept apparent disorder: The criminal is prosecuted, the lonely find love, the innocent child is cured. A landscape artist balances a random tree here, a river there, and a mountain far away with ordered composition. Our ears fill with constant arbitrary sounds, but a musician orders them into successive, abstract, and comprehensive tones.

The events in our lives are chaos. First we work devotedly at our jobs; then we date Mr./Ms. Right; then we paint the living room; then we get fired from our job; then we attend a family reunion; then read a book, go on vacation, break up with Mr./Ms. Jerk, move to a new city, total the car, get a nose job, and rob a 7-Eleven. Chaotic, but realistic (well, maybe not the 7-Eleven part).

As the musician orders sound and the painter orders sight, playwrights order events. Rather than life's chaotic *x* happens, and then *y* happens, and then *z* happens, playwrights *make* X happen, *which causes* Y to happen, *so therefore* Z happens.

This basic order of events is the *plot*. One event follows another, and this chain of events has a beginning, middle, and end. Plot is the framework of the Aristotelian play. There is a unity to these events; in other words, no event is arbitrarily thrown in without reason. Events are chosen by the playwright to accelerate the forward momentum of the plot. This consistency is what Aristotle called "Unity of Action."

The difference between an event and an action is the same as the difference between a loop and a chain: A chain is composed of many intertwined metal loops. Individually, these loops are without structure, but as soon as two are linked, they begin a chain. A play's action is an individual loop; an event is composed of an action that directly leads to or causes a subsequent action. That subsequent action links to another action until this consequential chain of events shapes a plot.

Not all actions in a play are part of an event. When *Betrayal's* Emma reaches for a sip of wine, it is an isolated action (or activity). But when Mr. Gibbs from *Arsenic and Old Lace* reaches for a sip of wine—which is laced with poison—it causes Mortimer to scream; which causes Gibbs to drop the glass; which makes Mortimer chase him out of the house; which causes the murderous aunts to scold Mortimer, who then confronts them about their dastardly hobby; which makes, causes, triggers, and snowballs every successive event until the play reaches its climax. In the two examples, the wine-sipping actions are identical; what constitutes one as an event is that it sparks another action. This is *plot*.

From Foundation to Rooftop

When exactly does the play *begin*? The plot, like any chain, has a beginning, but it does not necessarily begin when the lights come up.

According to science, the world was a mass of Periodic Table elements until an unexplained phenomenon triggered the first DNA. This created single-celled life, which evolved into multicelled life, which evolved into sentient life forms. In Judeo-Christian philosophy, there was only nothingness until God created the heavens and earth. This triggered His creation of a world, and in this world He then created light and darkness and living creatures. But without that first "spark," whether it was God's first creative day or serendipitous chemical reaction, the universe would have remained in balance as either stagnant elements or eternal nothingness forever.

Balance Every Aristotelian play begins in a state of balance that identifies which part of our chaotic world it's going to show. It is a balance because, peaceful or painful, it will go on without change forever. It can be as easy as William Inge's quiet little *Bus Stop* in Kansas, as turbulent as *Oedipus Rex*'s plague-ridden Thebes, or as bizarre as Kaufman and Hart's oddball family in *You Can't Take It with You*. Regardless, their balance would remain—built of quiet, turbulent, bizarre, and isolated actions—until one action triggers another and begins linking a chain of events.

The balance of Lorraine Hansberry's *A Raisin in the Sun* establishes the poverty-level circumstances of the Younger family.

> *Weariness has, in fact, won in this room. Everything has been polished, washed, sat on, used, and scrubbed too often. All pretenses but living itself have long since vanished from the very atmosphere of this room. . . . The single window that has been provided for those "two" rooms is located in the kitchen area. The sole natural light the family may enjoy in the course of a day is only that which lights its way through this little window.*
>
> *At rise: It is morning dark in the living room. TRAVIS is asleep on the make-down bed at center. An alarm clock sounds and RUTH enters from the bedroom. As she passes her sleeping son she reaches down and shakes him a little. She fills a pot with water and puts it on to boil. She calls to the boy, between yawns, in a slightly muffled voice.*

RUTH: I say hurry up, Travis! You ain't the only person in the
    world got to use a bathroom.

As her son exits out the apartment's front door to the shared bathroom in the hallway, we observe the morning routine and relationships of the five family members sharing the small, three-room
apartment. That is, until the next element.

Ignition The phenomenon that triggered DNA, the decision to create
a world out of nothingness, or the spark that lights an explosive's fuse
is the first link of that chain. In plot, it is the *ignition*. This is the "no
turning back" action that unstoppably alters that balance, *the* pebble
that starts the avalanche. After identifying the balance of the play's
initial world, pinpoint the ignition that propels the play forward.

    Euripides' *Medea* opens with her children's nurse explaining the
story (I'll discuss *exposition* next). Medea, who has abandoned and
betrayed her homeland in order to marry Jason here in Corinth, has
learned she has been betrayed by him when he announces his intention to marry the Corinthian king's daughter. Medea's suicidal
state is described by the nurse:

> She does not eat,
> lies prostrate, slumped in anguish,
> wastes away in day-long tears.
> Ever since she heard of Jason's perfidy
> she has not raised her eyes
> or looked up from the floor.

The balance is Medea's depressive state, her ex-husband's new marriage, and the chorus of Corinthian women's worry. This *would* have
continued indefinitely. But then Medea enters in anguish. When finally alone with the chorus, she attempts to ally them through
shared frustration. As women, they are powerless hostages to their
husbands' whims and desires. When she believes she has their
complete sympathy, she confides:

> So, please, I ask you this:
> if I can find a way to pay my husband back—
> your silence.

Here, Medea vows revenge, and this is the event that ignites the
play's forward action, the first link in the chain. As the King and

Jason confront her, she secretly constructs her plot to exact the most hideous vengeance. The script starts with the introduction of the story and characters, but the play begins when Medea swears revenge.

When does Tennessee Williams' *A Streetcar Named Desire* actually begin? The script starts with the general sounds and chatter of a court-yard in New Orleans' French Quarter. Stella and Stanley Kowalski tease each other as he goes off bowling with his buddies. The sounds, banter, and music in this two-page scene establish the balance. Then a woman, her delicate white dress in sharp contrast to her earthy surroundings, enters carrying a valise:

> *She looks at a slip of paper, then at the building, then again at the slip and again at the building. Her expression is one of shocked disbelief.*

The mere arrival of Blanche Dubois is an ignition. Her intrusion on this balanced world has the same igniting impact as the clad-in-black outlaw bursting through the saloon's swinging doors.

The ignition is not always near the beginning. In Molière's *Tartuffe*, a family is upended by the presence of a hypocritical religious zealot welcomed by the gullible father. The daughter, who was engaged to her true love, is now promised to Tartuffe. In a last ditch effort to change the tunnel-visioned father, the family appeals to his mother. She turns out to be as blindly loyal to her son as he is to Tartuffe. She becomes enraged that the family would question her son's judgment and exits in a fury. This is where the lights come up; Madame Pernell, the grandmother, is hurriedly rushing out:

> MADAME PERNELLE: Come, Come, Flipote [her personal maid]; it's
>   time I left this place!
> ELMIRE [the mother]: I can't keep up, you walk at such a pace.
> MADAME PERNELLE: Don't trouble, child; no need to show me out.
>   It's not your manners I'm concerned about.
> ELMIRE: We merely pay you the respect we owe.
>   But Mother, why this hurry? Must you go?
> MADAME PERNELLE: I must. This house appalls me. No one in it
>   Will pay attention for a single minute.
>   Children, I take my leave much vexed in spirit.
>   I offer advice, but you won't hear it.
>   You all break in and chatter on and on.
>   It's like a madhouse with the keeper gone!

If the balance of the play is a happy French family in which the daughter is soon to be wed to her beloved fiancé, then what is the ignition that disrupts this balance? In this case, when the father brings Tartuffe into this home with overindulged authority, his action triggers the family to rebel. And this happens before the script even begins! Imagine this doddering woman running out of the house followed by her maidservant, her grandson, her daughter-in-law, and the daughter-in-law's brother. Molière's plays begin in frenzy with the fuse already well-ignited.

Patrick Meyer's *K-2* is about two amateur mountain climbers whose rope has snapped, causing them to plunge down to an eight-by-four-foot ice shelf. One has broken a leg, and there is not enough rope for both to return to safety. The script opens seconds after the fall. Here, too, the ignition occurs before the lights come up.

The balance acts as an introduction or a preface; the ignition announces the true beginning, Chapter 1.

Exposition The proper phrase for *exposition*, for those who like *proper phrases*, is "antecedent action," which means the action has happened antecedent to (preceding) the action of the play. It is the information you need in order to know what's going on, just as if you'd walked in late with bucketfuls of popcorn and asked, "What have I missed so far?"

The argument between Madame Pernelle and her family includes exposition about Tartuffe: how he arrived, and who is involved. The nurse offers exposition about what happened to Medea so far.

Some exposition is more blatant than others. Tom Stoppard wrote a satire of British murder-mysteries called *The Real Inspector Hound*. He pokes fun at the obvious exposition of these drawing-room plays when Mrs. Drudge, the maid, answers the phone:

> Mrs. Drudge: Hello, the drawing room of Lady Muldoon's country residence one morning in early Spring. . . .

Not all obvious exposition is poor. Addressing the audience directly with the exposition is expedient and has been part of playwriting since the early Greeks. For example, the prologue to Christopher Marlowe's *Doctor Faustus*:

Only this, Gentles—we must now perform
The form of Faustus' fortunes, good or bad:
And now to patient judgments we appeal,
And speak for Faustus in his infancy.
Now is he born, of parents base of stock,
In Germany, within a town call'd Rhodes:
In riper years, to Wittenberg he went,
Whereas his kinsman chiefly brought him up.

Another more popular example of exposition is the *Brady Bunch* theme song in which we learn (every week) about a man raising three boys on his own and a lovely lady . . .

Contemporary realistic drama requires more subtlety. In James Goldman's *The Lion in Winter*, a historically based play that requires much exposition to establish history and character, the opening scene includes:

ALAIS [the king's mistress]: How is your queen?
HENRY: Decaying I suppose.
ALAIS: You haven't seen her?
HENRY: No, nor smelled nor touched nor tasted. Don't be jealous
   of the gorgon; she is not among the things I love. How many
   husbands do you know who dungeon up their wives? I
   haven't kept the great bitch in the keep for ten years out of
   passionate attachment . . .

In four exchanges, we learn that (1) Alais is envious; (2) Henry is indifferent to his wife's condition; (3) The Queen has been imprisoned for ten years; and (4) Henry loathes her.

In my play, *An Alternate Recipe*, a woman comes home late to find a still-set table with candles burnt to the nub. She asks her slumping roommate, "Where's tall, dark, and married?" This establishes in image and five words the exposition necessary for the scene.

The challenge for actors is to make exposition active. The simplistic choice is to relate the information because "the audience needs to know this." But the simplest choices are also the most boring. Madame Pernelle *lambastes* her son's family. The Corinthian women *beseech* the gods to help Medea. Playing a prologue may seem more difficult, but it is actually a white canvas on which you can paint a character, a relationship with the audience, and a purpose for relaying all this information. You might want to excite the crowd about this play you adore. You may need to elicit their sympathies or to manipulate their opinions to agree with yours. A well-played prologue can be a thrilling moment that gears the audience for what is to follow, much like a good movie promo makes you say, "I gotta see that!"

If exposition is *within* the play's plot, identify in which link of the *events chain* this exposition falls. Once you understand how this information accelerates the plot, you will play it unaware of the dialogue's utility.

Climax Life's rhythms are stresses and releases. The moon exerts a gravitational pull on the tides that builds stress until they are released by the rotation of the earth. The tectonic plates of the earth, constantly moving, build stress until they release violently on fault lines. Your heart beats with rapid stresses and releases, as your breathing stresses and releases your lungs. The faster you breathe, the more stress your body reflects or exerts. People relish release and even like to heighten the sensation through delayed gratification. Christmas morning for children (and a few of us adults) is an exhilarating release of weeks of gloriously stressful anticipation. Sex is perhaps the most primal example; the act of creating life is an intense build-up of stress until an explosive release.

This ultimate release of stress in a script—as in life—is the *climax*. Drama thrives on conflict. The intensifying stresses and releases within the plot build up pressure like a covered pot boiling rapidly and spouting bursts of steam until it finally explodes. The script's opposing forces pressurize to the point that an ultimate, final victory is imperative for only one. That event is the climax.

A climax can be defined by a number of criteria. The first can be the *climax of action*, such as Stanley Kowalski's rape of Blanche Dubois. In fact, Stanley defines dramatic climax: "You and me have had this date with each other from the beginning."

Another can be the *climax of idea*, such as Eliza Doolittle's assertion that she is independent of Professor Higgins' control in Shaw's *Pygmalion*:

> ELIZA: Wring away. What do I care? I knew you'd strike me some
> day. Aha! Now I know how to deal with you. What a fool I
> was not to think of it before! You can't take away the
> knowledge you gave me. You said I had a finer ear than you.

> And I can be civil and kind to people, which is more than you
> can. Aha! That's done you 'enry 'iggins, it 'az. . . . Oh, when I
> think of myself crawling under your feet and being trampled
> on and called names when all the time I had only to lift up my
> finger to be as good as you, I could just kick myself.

In classically based tragedy, it is a *climax of recognition* (Greek word:
anagnorsis). Lillian Hellman's *The Children's Hour* is about two 1934
school teachers/owners whose lives are destroyed by a child's unjus-
tified "accusation" that they are lesbians. In the climactic scene,
Martha recognizes the dormant truth behind the lie:

> MARTHA: I've been telling myself since the night we heard the
> child say it; I've been praying I could convince myself of it. I
> can't, I can't any longer. It's there. I don't know how, I don't
> know why. But I did love you. I do love you. I resented your
> marriage; maybe because I wanted you, maybe I wanted you
> all along; maybe I couldn't call it by a name; maybe it's been
> there ever since I first knew you. . . . I've ruined your life. I've
> ruined my own. I didn't even know. There's a big difference
> between us now, Karen. I feel all dirty and—I can't stay with
> you anymore. . . .

Regardless of type, the sequence of stresses and releases within the
script build to the final showdown, payoff, victory, or punch line:
the climax.

Resolution After an earthquake, television cameras in helicopters
pan over the ruins. They take in the entirety of the locale: Smolder-
ing fires dot the streets, structures lay in ruins, sirens reverberate
from miles around. After climactic events, human nature wants to
scan the outcome. The image of walking barefoot through carpets
of lottery-won money is a cliché describing the desire to survey the
entirety of the win. Pizza jaunts after opening night allow the performers to look back at the total culmination of all their hard work.
These are forms of closure or completion.

Without closure we feel uncomfortable, just like when we hear
a radio song that gets cut off before the last note. If you assemble a
thousand-piece jigsaw puzzle that only came with 999 or leave a
tied ballgame at the bottom of the ninth, you recognize the frustration of missing closure. If a friend moves out of town without say-

ing good-bye, if a close relative dies unexpectedly, or if a baby is taken from you for adoption without your seeing its face, then you experience the pain of incompletion.

The building stresses in a play are an exertion not only for the performers but also for the audience. After identifying with the characters and emerging from the climax, the audience wants to survey the ruins or celebrate in their victory. This post-climax event is the *resolution*. Proper phrases here are *denouement*, which is French for "untying the knot," or *falling action*, which logically follows a climax of *rising action*.

The resolution usually establishes a new balance, which can be the restoration of the initial one or a change to a better (or worse) balance. After the climax of *A Streetcar Named Desire*, Blanche, who is no longer able to endure the cruelties of life, is committed to a mental institution, but the balance of the French Quarter courtyard is restored. In Giraudaux's *The Madwoman of Chaillot*, the evil capitalists are imprisoned in the Paris sewer system, and so a new and better balance is created. In Edward Albee's *Who's Afraid of Virginia Woolf?*, George and Martha are devastated, stripped of their protective armor, and terrified of the new world they have reached. But they finally find each other—and this balance, although unendurably painful, is a highly optimistic new beginning, a salvaging balance.

Everything in the script that follows the climax is the resolution. Some scripts give "false climaxes" to lure you into believing you're free and clear, only to jolt you with a more powerful moment. Steven Spielberg is a master at creating scripts like this. In contrast, some action films end immediately after the climax; all you need to know is that everyone lives (or dies), which is enough to imply a new balance.

Framing the Masculine Structure
Balance, exposition, rising actions and events, climax, and resolution have evolved from Aristotle's outline for play composition. This masculine structure unifies all the script's actions to fuel the ultimate climactic event. Digressions from this focus weaken the play as they interrupt the momentum toward the climax.

When analyzing a masculine script, frame the shape of its structure with the events chain. What follows is an example using Shakespeare's *Romeo and Juliet* broken down into its structural elements.

Exposition

> PROLOGUE: Two households both alike in Dignity,
> In Fair Verona where we lay our scene . . .

The Houses of Capulet and Montague are embittered neighbors who have been feuding fiercely.

Balance

> PRINCE: If even you disturb our streets again,
> Your lives shall pay the forfeit of the peace . . .

The Prince decrees that the winner of the next duel fought to the death will be himself put to death, so the citizens of each house live in tense coexistence.

> ROMEO: Alas that love, whose view is muffled still,
> Should without eyes see pathways to his will . . .

Romeo, of the Montague house, is in love (again)—this time with Rosaline, whom he hardly knows and who has sworn to be chaste to her death. This balance would continue indefinitely with various plots by the two rivaled houses to provoke each other, and with various women who inspire the in-love-with-love Romeo until . . .

Ignition Depending on interpretation, two actions can be viewed as the ignition. The first interpretation: After Romeo's father asks his nephew Benvolio to help discover the cause of his son's depression, Benvolio endeavors to cure it.

> BENVOLIO [to Romeo]: At this same ancient feast of Capulet's
> Sups the fair Rosaline whom thou so loves,
> With all the admired beauties of Verona.
> Go thither, and with unattained eye,
> Compare her face with same that I shall show,
> And I will make thee think thy swan a crow.

Romeo reluctantly agrees to attend the feat, which prompts Benvolio to ready his cousin for meeting someone more worthy of his love than Rosaline, which triggers the doomed love affair with Juliet.

The second action that may be interpreted as the ignition: Pushed into attending the Capulet party, Romeo sees Juliet, a Capulet. Falling in love at first sight, he vows to meet her.

ROMEO: The measure done, I'll watch her place of stand,
  And touching hers make blessed my rude hand.
  Did my heart love 'til now? Forswear it sight,
  For I never saw true beauty 'til this night.

This triggers him to introduce himself to Juliet, which arouses her to fall in love with him.

If you interpret that Benvolio is strongly concerned about Romeo's depressed condition, then the first example represents a unique action that upsets the balance. If you feel Benvolio is accustomed to Romeo's love-sickness—and the Capulet party is one more distraction for his cousin as well as another opportunity to taunt the enemy house—then the second example is the ignition: Romeo's promise to meet Juliet, an adversary. Regardless of choice or interpretation, the igniting action must be the one that surpasses combustion threshold and ignites the flame.

The Events
From this point, trace each link of the chain that leads to the story's tragic climax:

- Romeo approaches Juliet.
- Juliet falls in love with Romeo.
- Insomniac Romeo sneaks into her garden to catch a glimpse of her.
- Juliet confesses her love to him.
- They pledge to marry in secret.
- Romeo solicits the help of Friar Lawrence to marry them.
- Juliet solicits the help of her nurse to further the plan.
- Friar Lawrence marries Juliet to Romeo.
- Mercutio and Benvolio, Romeo's friends, bump into Tybalt, Juliet's beloved but pugnacious cousin.
- Romeo stumbles onto their altercation.
- Romeo shows respect and affection to his new cousin.
- Mercutio, infuriated, challenges Tybalt to duel.
- Romeo attempts to stop it.
- With Romeo between them, Tybalt is able to kill Mercutio.
- Romeo kills Tybalt to avenge Mercutio.
- The Prince banishes Romeo.
- After his wedding night in Juliet's chamber, Romeo flees to Mantua.

- Juliet, betrothed to the nobleman Paris, pleads with her parents to postpone the wedding.
- Her father threatens to disown her if she does not follow through with the marriage.
- Juliet runs to Friar Lawrence for advice.
- Friar Lawrence gives Juliet a potion that will simulate death.
- The Friar sends details of their plan to Romeo.
- Juliet takes the drug.
- Juliet's nurse discovers her "dead" in the morning.
- Balthasar, Romeo's servant, races to Mantua with the news of Juliet's death and precedes the arrival of Friar Lawrence's report.
- Romeo returns to Verona to die with Juliet.
- Romeo breaks into the Capulet vault.
- The mourning Paris mistakes Romeo for a thief and fights him.
- Romeo kills Paris.

Climax The tensions build to the point that they can no longer endure without release.

- Romeo finds Juliet.
- He bids her farewell.
- He drinks poison.
- Friar Lawrence returns to the awakening Juliet.
- She discovers Romeo's body.
- Friar Lawrence begs Juliet to leave.
- She sends him away.
- She stabs herself with Romeo's dagger.

Resolution After both teenagers end their own lives, the tension is released. Those who remain alive, as well as the audience, scan the remains.

- The Prince struggles to understand what has happened.
- Romeo's mother dies of a broken heart.
- Friar Lawrence confesses the story.
- The Prince absolves the friar of blame.
- The Prince denounces Capulet, Montague, and himself for Romeo and Juliet's deaths.
- Capulet and Montague pledge truce.

Resolved Balance After the resolution, a new balance is established. It too will go unchanged until something else surpasses ignition temperature.

> *Two houses both alike in dignity,*
> *In fair Verona where we Lay our scene . . .*

now in harmony.

Part II: The Feminine Script

When Black American playwright Victor Séjour wrote his plays in the mid 1800s, they were about white aristocratic society. Does this mean that he didn't know or care anything about the black experience? Unlikely. It can be assumed he *did* know, however, that the theatre-going audience of his day was predominately white and uninterested in black culture, and that if he wanted his creations to be seen, they would have to appeal directly to that contemporary audience. Anton Chekhov was a physician, but he never wrote plays about the controversies in medical theories. Unlike novelists, playwrights must immediately and actively involve their audiences, reaching them through situations and language they relate to and understand.

Within the last hundred years, women began emerging as an equally dominant force. With any introduction of power, new forms of expression surface, and now uniquely feminine artistic structures prevail in Western civilization. This is not to say that these forms didn't exist. Certainly, women were expressing themselves in distinctly feminine ways before this century. However, since the selections for play production, novel publication, gallery showing, and so on, were being made overwhelmingly by men, these forms were either suppressed or lost over time.

Other than the obvious anatomical differences celebrated between the glossy pages of questionable magazines, there are hundreds of other contrasting qualities to the sexes. Current science has uncovered a variety of gender-specific differences. For example, women's wide-field vision is more accurate, yet men's night vision is stronger. Due to hip placement, men can run faster, yet women have more endurance. Females have better manual dexterity and males have better space relations. Males have more muscle mass whereas females have more fat reserves: strength versus stamina. When testosterone, a male hormone, is injected into female test animals, it produces markedly increased aggression. Estrogen, a female hormone, is directly responsible for synaptic responses in the brain. One could theorize that these differences evolved (or were created) for species survival—with females built to bear and protect children, and males to feed and secure the genetic line. Fortunately, civilization and technologies have made obsolete the physical restrictions that limit lifestyle choice.

The most primal example of our gender differences is apparent in sexual response. Contemporary research has shown that women express themselves sexually through their entire bodies, whereas men radiate that energy from their sexual organ. Most relevant to script analysis is this: Men are focused primarily on a climax, whereas women are focused on overall sensation. A woman can have a rewarding sexual experience without climax, and a man can have a rewarding experience with *nothing but* a climax. Each sex may also experience the energy of the opposite sex, since both qualities are present in varying degrees in both. However, each sex *generally* reacts with gender-specific responses.

The differences in our evolutionary development and our primal sexual responses help explain how what was commonly considered *effective* playwriting evolved as having a chain of events targeted toward achieving a purging climax. The primarily male audiences of Aristotle's time were naturally more moved by linear progressions to a final goal. Yet this is not the only structure that achieves a full, satisfying theatrical experience.

Feminine (Circular) Framework

If you were traveling by car from one coast to the other, you could do it two ways. The first: Get on Interstate 80, drive east or west until you hit an ocean—when you do, you're there. This should take about six days, but you'll only see lots of highway. Or, you can start heading east or west on one of a plethora of roads, stop to visit a town you've never seen, see a natural landmark, and maybe even "find out where this odd road goes." You'll get there anywhere from a few weeks to eleven years but see countless sights.

In the first method, the rewards are expediency, economy, and focus. In the second method, the rewards are experience, spontaneity, and discovery. Since it is not a requirement to pick only one method, most people employ bits of both. *The emphasis* depends on priority: Do you need to get there, or do you want an adventure? The masculine script emphasizes the goal; the feminine script emphasizes the experience.

While the masculine script emphasizes singular or parallel plot lines climaxed by a powerful event, the feminine script emphasizes the *process* of exploring a basic thematic idea through a succession of varied but equally weighted scene variations. What follows are the structural elements of the feminine script.

Subject For the scene variations to have continuity, they need unifying focus.

In Baroque music, a popular form perfected by Johann Sebastian Bach was called the *fugue*. Fugues are compositions with many voices, each treated with equal importance, each resonating its exploration of a given theme. That theme is usually a short melody line stated by any one voice at the fugue's beginning. That melody line is called the *subject*. In a fugue, the first thing you hear is that identifying subject; then you hear the *answer*, which is another voice interpreting that subject; and then others still added onto those. The fugue ends when the subject is fully expanded and the contrasting voices rejoin in unison. It's complex, intelligent, evolutionary, and engrossing.

The unifying force of the feminine script, like the fugue, is the *subject*. The subject is the concept or thematic idea(s) the playwright wishes to explore (see Chapter 11). It can be an observation about human behavior, a debate on social structure, an exploration of an emotion, or even the celebration of life's joy, as in a musical review. The subject of a feminine script says, "This is what we're talking about here," just as the subject of the fugue says, "This is the sound we're going to play with."

Susan Glaspell, a Pulitzer Prize–winning playwright from the first half of this century, wrote a short detective-story play about the investigation of a woman in 1916 who allegedly strangled her husband. However, we never see that woman, and the sheriff and D.A. who investigate are rarely on stage. Instead, we remain with the scouting men's wives in the suspected murderer's kitchen. Frequently, the men appear and discover the women looking through the cabinets trying to piece together the mindset of the alleged murderer. The men deride these women for their attention to trivialities when their *own* concentrations are so much more important. Yet the women, to their horror, are the ones to uncover the tangible evidence leading toward a motive necessary for conviction. In the last scene, as the men ridicule the women for their attention to "trivial" details, the women—who identify with the wife's unbearable circumstances—conceal the evidence. The play's subject is identified through its ironic title: *Trifles*.

The thematic idea of this play is not "trifles are important, too," but that the delineation of what is trifling and what is essential has been deleteriously off balance; if women's priorities were weighted equally with men's priorities, the result could be a richer world. Glaspell dramatizes this by having her characters solve a murder only through confronting "trifles." The audience is privileged to join these characters in the kitchen and share their insights.

The "plot" of *Trifles*, as defined by Aristotelian structure, happens offstage and is basically irrelevant. The scenes that are relevant involve the domestic activities of the women while they wait for the men to finish the "important" work. There is no building chain of events and certainly no climax. The strongest dialogue is spoken without words. But in the real waiting time of the play, the questions are answered, the motive is revealed, and the circle is completed.

Like *Trifles*, the subject is often reflected in the title of a feminine script. *Uncommon Women and Others*, by Wendy Wasserstein, is about five alumnae who reunite six years after graduation. Through flashbacks, they struggle to make sense of how their hopes manifested in choices. Kate, a successful corporate attorney, says in the final scene: "I guess it never occurred to me in college that someone wouldn't want me to be quite so uncommon."

Through flashbacks unhindered by Aristotelian plot, Wasserstein weaves the stories of five uncommon women's development, processes, and victories. The flashback plots are episodic and without explosive climax, but the processes of each woman's four-year college development juxtaposed against their progress six years later completes the circular picture.

Unlike the ignition of a linear script, the subject of a circular script doesn't have to be stated at the script's opening or in the title (although it often is). In fact, if the subject is considered difficult to swallow, it might even be best left until the end. Jean Genet's *The*

Balcony is about a high-class brothel going about business as usual during a bloody revolution. Through a series of, shall we say, "atypical" sessions, we see laborers acting out graphic fantasies as statesmen: Judge, Bishop, and General. However, with the country in revolution, the "real" leaders have been assassinated and the Chief of Police (the Madame's insecure lover) publicly parades these clients in costume to establish solidarity again. (For good measure, the Madame impersonates the Queen.) The revolution's heroic leader is really a plumber. The Bishop is a gas man. The brothel is called "A House of Illusion." The play's subject is ultimately identified when Irma, the Madame, addresses the audience directly: "You must now go home where everything—you can be quite sure—will be falser than here . . .

Topic Variations To construct a house, you have to begin with the foundation and build to the roof. To construct a jigsaw puzzle, you can begin with *any* two pieces that match. The house construction requires linear progression (gravity is tough to overcome). Puzzle construction requires relationships between varying pieces and can be constructed in any sequence. The feminine script is like a jigsaw puzzle.

The scenes within the circular script are *the topic variations*. Each topic variation examines an angle or point of view on the thematic subject. When the variations are pieced together in complementary relationship to each other, the entire picture is created.

The circular script's variations do not utilize Aristotle's tidy Unities. Instead of those sequential action/trigger/action events, the script layers variation upon variation through diverse scenes and devices. Since topic variations don't have to follow the logic of time or unified action (plot), the notes played and instruments used are unlimited—constricted only by necessary thematic consistency.

For example, Sam Shepard wrote a play with Joseph Chaikin called *Savage/Love*. The subject is stated immediately in the title. The scenes within the play are also titled. Some of these are: "First Moment," "Tangled Up," "Terms of Endearment," "Killing," "Beggar," "How I Look to You," "The Hunt," "Watching the Sleeping Lover." Shepard and Chaikin wanted to explore the conflicting ecstasy and anguish of nonromanticized love. A linear exploration of a specific plot would have been too logical and neat for their chaotic statement. Instead, they focus the audience on the subject through the title and add piece relating to piece until their bipolar picture is complete.

Jane Martin's *Talking With* . . . illuminates American women through an enormous variety of characters: a woman rodeo rustler, a backwoods snake handler, a leading lady in her dressing room, an any-minute-now mother in the throes of labor, a self-mutilating baton twirler, among others. These characters could scarcely be believable together in one or two plot lines without enormous and awkward machination. But by focusing on an assembly that comes full circle rather than on a beginning-middle-end, Martin can use a wide range of characters in disparate circumstances that merge to make a full vision.

Waiting for Lefty was Clifford Odets' first play before he "studied" traditional playwriting. Its titled topic variations paint a portrait of abused labor and failing American democracy during the Depression: "Joe and Edna," a marriage being destroyed; "The Young Hack and His Girl," young lovers who cannot afford to get married; "The Lab Assistant Episode," an employee threatened into espionage; "Interne Episode," a doctor fired because of prejudice. The play is concise and powerful without needing to justify a coincidental relationship between the characters or to weave an intricate plot line for unity.

Since the circular script does not rely on chronology, one way to recognize this structure is to determine if you can transpose the order of scenes without losing integrity. Obviously, the playwright orders the scenes for artistic reasons and they *shouldn't be monkeyed with*, but in the overall understanding of the play, cause-and-effect sequence is less crucial than thematic relationship and counterpoint.

Although Maria Irene Fornes' *Fefu and Her Friends* implies a plot chronology, the play's images would stand up almost as well if they were totally inverted. The sketchy plot, secondary to its thematic impact, is that Fefu and her college buddies meet to prepare for an effective-education fundraiser. However, that preparation turns out to be little more than a cursory rehearsal. Instead, the diverse relationships between these women and the effects that subjugation to male ideology has had on them are paramount. These variation scenes need not be in sequence and, in fact, are sequentially different for each of four audience groups as outlined below.

Part I: Noon. The living room. The entire audience watches from the main auditorium.
Part II: Afternoon. The lawn, the study, the bedroom, the kitchen.

> *The audience is divided into four groups. Each group is led to the spaces. Those scenes are performed simultaneously. When the scenes are completed the audience moves to the next space and the scenes are performed again. This is repeated four times until each group has seen all four scenes. Then the audience is led back to the main auditorium. Part III: Evening. The living room. The audience watches from the main auditorium.*

Does this mean only one section of the audience watches it in the "right" order? Or does it mean that the chronological order is irrelevant and that the relationship to the simultaneously occurring events, in whatever sequence, is the focus? You can enter a skating rink at any point and still complete the same circle.

A Chorus Line, a musical about seventeen dancers competing for eight Broadway jobs, hangs its topic variations on the general beginning-middle-end of an audition. However, the character-study scenes about each auditioner are the prime focus. In fact, at the play's end, even though only eight are cast, all seventeen—including the casting choreographer/director—perform the finale as though the potential "climax" of who gets the jobs is unimportant. The subject—the unique beauty and nobility of individuals choosing to be one of a whole—is expressed in the song "What I Did for Love." The variations are scenes, songs, and dances performed by each of the seventeen "gypsies." If any of these pieces were relocated to other places, the show, although artistically weakened, would still fully communicate and explore its topic.

Completion A line stops when it reaches its endpoint; in linear writing, that endpoint is the resolution. A circle is complete when it is closed; in circular writing, that closing point is the *completion*. Instead of offering a climactic showdown, the circular script ends with a satisfying totality similar to the feeling you have when you finish viewing a museum collection. There is a sense of fulfillment, saturation, and entirety. You could view longer, but additional information becomes superfluous, overkill. All the parts have merged into one experience.

As with any circle, the "end" cannot be pinpointed. You cannot point to the "completion scene" (the way you can identify a linear script's climax) anymore than you could spot the last piece of the jigsaw puzzle. However, at the circular script's finish, that satisfying fulfillment is *felt*. When the playwright or fugue composer has explored as many variations as he or she needs—or *senses*—to complete the work, the play or composition is over. If they are successful, completion is achieved. If they have fallen short, the audience is left frustrated, confused, or unsatisfied.

By the end of Glaspell's *Trifles*, you feel an enormous satisfaction—not only because the murder was solved by piecing together a puzzle, but also because of the concise exploration of another way to experience the world: through the attention paid to our daily lives' subtle details.

At the conclusion of *Uncommon Women and Others*, you feel a bond to these women, as they feel toward each other. You also gain a deep understanding of the struggles they have had to emerge whole in a society that dictates they only be part.

Through Shepard and Chaikin's *Savage/Love*, you recognize the utter chaos and contradiction of intimate relationships; you feel like you've spent an hour inside a clothes dryer. Fornes' *Fefu and Her Friends* completes its complex circle with the hope that women can free themselves from thousands of years of social oppression. After its short hours and through its microcosm of contemporary women, the audience sees a complete picture of entrapment, revolt, rally, battle, and victory. *A Chorus Line* ennobles these gypsy dancers so much that you want to leave your chair and join them as equals during their grand, celebratory finale.

Framing the Feminine Structure

When you break down a circular script into its workable parts, focus first on the overall concept or theme and then outline the topic variations which explore that idea.

Caryl Churchill, a contemporary British playwright, is a master of this structure. What follows is a breakdown of her *Top Girls*. Unlike the rigidly defined elements of a linear script, a circular script allows much more variety and requires a great deal of subjective interpretation. *Theme in the circular script takes precedence over action; idea is more important than event.*

Note: Since themes and ideas are highly subjective, it is important to remember that the following breakdown is only one perspective for analyzing the Churchill play. More important than the subjective conclusions below is understanding the process by which they were reached.

Subject The subject is reflected in the title; the play explores the heritage and achievements of great women or "top girls"—the obstacles they overcome, the crucial ingredients for success, and the sacrifices that often need to be made. Instead of concentrating on the loudly heroic figures commonly defined by traditional histori- ans as great women (Joan of Arc, Queen Elizabeth I, Eleanor Roo- sevelt, and others), Churchill celebrates quieter though no less heroic ("*Trifle?*") victors. There are no male characters, and the play confronts the interactions, obstacles, and support great women have for and against each other in order to achieve their goals.

The Variations The play's variation scenes can be assembled in a number of sequences without compromising the play's impact. The BBC television adaptation opened with the interview of Act II (scene 3) of the play, yet the script was equally powerful. Churchill notes at the beginning of the script:

> *Top Girls* was originally written in three acts and I understand that structure clearer: Act One, the dinner; Act Two, Angie's story; Act Three, the year before. But two intervals do hold things up, so in the original production we made it two acts with the interval after what is here Act Two, scene two. Do whichever you prefer.

Act I: Using little-known historical and fictional women juxtaposed against a contemporary achiever, Act I addresses the history and heritage of great women in civilization. In a surreal victory dinner, five diverse women join Marlene in celebrating her promotion as executive for the "Top Girls Employment Agency." The women with Marlene are:

> Isabella Bird: an independent traveler from the nineteenth cen- tury.
>
> Lady Nijo: a thirteenth-century Japanese emperor's courtesan.
>
> Dull Gret: a fictional battler from a sixteenth-century Brueghel painting.
>
> Pope Joan: a nineth-century woman who, disguised as a man, was elected pope for two years.
>
> Patient Griselda: fictional fourteenth-century wife from Chaucer's *Canterbury Tales*.

As the six women drink steadily, they recount their differing but similarly sacrificing life stories. They sympathize, compete, diminish, and
support each other. Overlapping conversations, listening and talking
simultaneously, accepting and rejecting, they ultimately embrace Marlene into their fold of independent and outstanding Top Girls.

Act II: Act II's topic variations explore the processes, evolution, resources, and talents necessary to create and become a great woman.
A failing of courage, talent, background, or choice is enough to
stunt a potential into mediocrity.

- Scene 1: Marlene interviews a client who wants to advance
  her career with an eye on advertising. Yet she also hopes to
  get married and have children. *The choice to do both means a
  compromise in each.* She is sent out for two disappointing job
  prospects with knitwear and lampshade manufacturers.
- Scene 2: Angie, Marlene's niece, hides in the yard with her
  much younger neighborhood friend, Kit. Angie plots with
  Kit to leave her mother's house and build an independent
  life. What starts with plans to sneak to a movie ends with
  Angie's plot to murder her mother, Joyce. She denies her,
  imagining that her Aunt Marlene is her real mother. Joyce
  tries to lure Angie inside with alternating threats, kind-
  nesses, and insults. Kit brags to Joyce about her aspiration
  of becoming a nuclear physicist while Angie wields a brick
  as a murder weapon. Yet she is unable to carry through. She
  stands alone in the rain, brick in hand, as Kit points out her
  failure. *Lack of courage, intelligence, or determination paralyze
  her dreams.*
- Scene 3: Win and Nell, two Top Girls Agency employees, discuss their weekends. One is having an affair with a married
  man; the other's boyfriend has proposed to her again. The
  newly promoted Marlene arrives, joining them in spirit but
  not in gossip. They congratulate her, yet it is also clear that
  they are no longer equals.
- Interview: Win interviews a woman who, after twenty-one
  years with the same company, seeks advancement. She relates her invaluable contribution to that company, the sacrifices in her personal life, and the frustration of watching
  less-qualified men whom she trained surpass her. *In a failed*

attempt to pass as a man in behavior, she has lost her goals and her self.

- Main Office: Angie arrives unexpectedly in Marlene's office with no more plans than to live with her aunt. They are interrupted by Mrs. Kidd's arrival, who is the wife of the man Marlene beat out for promotion. The wife reveals that Mr. Kidd is so shaken by his failure that he is bedridden. She attempts to persuade Marlene to step down. When this fails, she attacks Marlene's femininity. When *the wife calls her "unnatural," Marlene tells the woman to "piss off."* Angie revels in her aunt's power, but Marlene is visibly shaken.
- Interview: Nell interviews Shona, a young woman of seemingly extraordinary capacity. This woman seems to be a young Marlene, with intelligence, early success, independence, and assertion. It becomes clear, however, that she is more likely a future Angie, *a dull dreamer without the resources to manifest them into achievement.*
- Main Office: Win meets Angie, who is awaiting her Aunt Marlene. Win begins to relate the arduous process of self-discovery and struggle that led to her current stature. Angie, who prompted her originally, nods off somewhere in the middle of it. Marlene enters and, *seeing Angie, sentences her: "She's not going to make it."*

Act III: The third act, set one year earlier, focuses on the sacrifices, crossroads, and turning points of every woman's path to full potential. The results of these options create sexual classes and subclasses. Choice is juxtaposed with circumstance as the act reveals the similarities and differences of these sisters that led to their sharply contrasting lives.

- In Joyce's kitchen, Angie has invited her aunt to visit for the first time in six years under the pretense that Joyce has asked her to do so. The tension of this reunion is heavy. It is revealed that Angie is truly Marlene's daughter whom Joyce took in as her own because Joyce was married and believed she couldn't bear children. In this confrontation, universal topics of choice and situation arise.
- Marlene defines the requirements:

MARLENE: Anyone can do anything if they've got what it
  takes.
JOYCE: And if they haven't?
MARLENE: If they're stupid, lazy or frightened, I'm not going to
  help them get a job. Why should I?

■ Angie celebrates Marlene's arrival in a way that demonstrates
  her inherent limitations. Marlene denies recognition of Angie's
  limits.

MARLENE [to Angie]: Do you want to work with children?
JOYCE: She's not clever like you.
(Pause.)
MARLENE: I'm not clever, just pushy.
JOYCE: True enough.

> The domestic choices are explored: Joyce's marriage, which
> has dissolved; a woman they knew whose husband, learning
> she was having an affair with a young man, murdered her;
> their mother, who is finishing her life in a nursing home.
> About their occasionally lucid mother, Marlene says, "Fucking
> awful life she's had . . . fucking waste."

■ Joyce, who did get pregnant after taking Angie, lost her baby
  because of the enormous demands of her sister's infant. Marlene questions whether it would be possible to have children
  herself. Joyce blames Marlene; Marlene accuses her of jealousy. They fight for the one child between them.

MARLENE: . . . I don't want a baby. I don't want to talk about
  gynecology.
JOYCE: Then stop trying to get Angie off me.

■ Tears and apologies bring out the bonds between sisters. This
  erupts when Marlene celebrates the new election of Margaret
  Thatcher, an opinion Joyce views as blindly feminist. The rift
  between the classes becomes a metaphor for the rift between
  women of different pursuits and capabilities. Marlene hates
  the working class—laborers and their wives or mothers—
  which represents the family from which she escaped. Joyce
  hates the wealthy—selfish achievers who leave family neces-
  sities to others—and points out that Marlene's escape left a
  child who required care.

JOYCE: I suspect her [Angie's] children will say what a wasted life she had . . . because nothing's changed and won't with them [Thatcher's party].

MARLENE: Them. Us and them.

JOYCE: And you're one of them.

MARLENE: And you're us, wonderful us, and Angie's us, and Mum and Dad's us.

Like the classes, the rift is unresolvable. They cannot be friends. There cannot be apologies. *Women have created subclasses independent of male influence.* They part unresolved.

Completion

ANGIE: Mum?

MARLENE: No, she's gone to bed. It's Aunty Marlene.

ANGIE: Frightening.

MARLENE: Did you have a bad dream? What happened in it? Well, you're awake now, aren't you pet?

ANGIE: Frightening.

By the play's conclusion, summarized by this final scene, you recognize a complete picture of the complicated path of women's achievement. Unlike men's, it is compounded by the real and complex draw of motherhood. In a world whose means for triumph have been outlined by the sex without this option, women's achievements require adaptation and sacrifice, which also creates a class system within the sex. The minimum requirements—intelligence, active will, and courage—are too often impossible for too many. The topics are explored in enough variations to illuminate clearly the many facets of a complex vision; Churchill's circle is complete.

Contrasting the Masculine and Feminine

The masculine script is linear. It has a clear beginning, middle, and end. Each point on that line can be identified by its function (see Figure 1–1).

The feminine script circles a theme with topic variations that complete a full picture (see Figure 1–2).

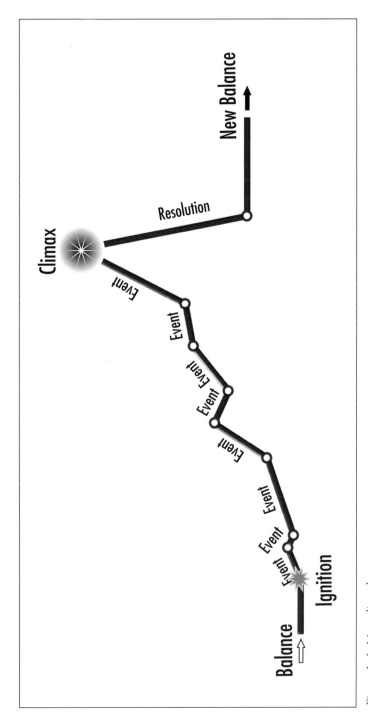

Figure 1–1 Masculine plot

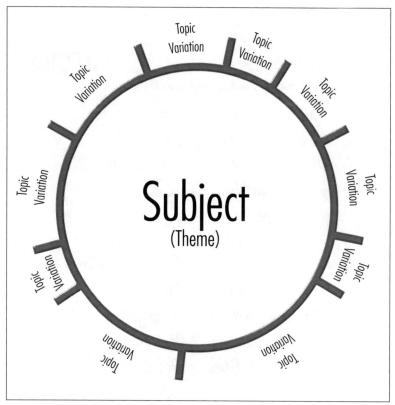

Figure 1–2   Feminine plot

Note the comparison of the two viewpoints using specific and abstract elements and concepts (see Figure 1–3).

"Judging" the success of a script (for those insistent on judging works of art) is more complicated for feminine script aspects because of their subjective nature. Masculine script elements can be broken down easily into distinct steps. Feminine script elements have fewer rules and more options. The effectiveness of the masculine script can be measured by the successful, unified completion of its steps—no loose ends, exciting climax, and character journey. The effectiveness of the feminine script is measured by the satisfying wholeness felt at the final curtain. If the subject has not been fully explored, then the script falls short. If it has made a strong impression and created a full experience, then it achieves its goal.

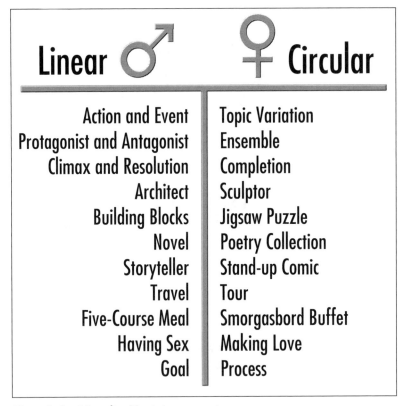

Linear ♂	♀ Circular
Action and Event	Topic Variation
Protagonist and Antagonist	Ensemble
Climax and Resolution	Completion
Architect	Sculptor
Building Blocks	Jigsaw Puzzle
Novel	Poetry Collection
Storyteller	Stand-up Comic
Travel	Tour
Five-Course Meal	Smorgasbord Buffet
Having Sex	Making Love
Goal	Process

Figure 1–3   Masculine/Feminine comparison

Very often critics have adjudicated scripts as being ineffective because they have looked only for the familiar elements of linear progression. It is up to the performers and directors to show that our world is not limited to one viewpoint. But this requires a clear understanding of the tools. Actors who impose linear build on circular constructions weaken the collage of topic variations. Actors who place equal weight on all events of linear construction as though they were topic variations rob the thrusting momentum of events that build to climax.

2 Truth in Action

At the very least, theatre requires audience involvement on an emotional, intellectual, or physical level. In order for audiences to connect with what is happening onstage, they must identify with the characters or recognize that something real—truthful—is happening in front of them. Since the great majority of plays portray real characters in given circumstances—even if expressed abstractly—then the behavior of those characters must be recognizable to the real people in the audience. For this reason, you must make yourself a student of human behavior.

A crucial element of human behavior that was once thought to be unique to our species is *language*. We speak to each other, to our gods, to our pets, to our plants, to traffic—to anything that will listen. Scripts are chiefly composed of dialogue, and certainly that dialogue is the most important element in the vast majority of theatre. Look at the difference between how stage plays and film plays are printed. Films are about images—they have their roots in moving pictures—and thus the margins of descriptions are wide and featured, and the dialogue is offset in narrower margins. But plays feature dialogue that is bold and wide on the page, with stage directions restrained to a minimum, offset in italicized, narrow margins.

The Prime Rule of Acting Dialogue

Before telling you a basic concept for acting dialogue, I need to fill you in on a little background that may seem totally irrelevant but will make sense afterward. Promise.

Of all animals, we are one of the most helpless when born. We have laughable muscle control, no practical use of our senses, and no instincts. But we can make a lot of noise. I have three nieces, and I have never heard such massive sounds coming from such compact speakers. This tool evolved to communicate our survival needs with our parents. It works.

Babies cry for one of three reasons: (1) they want food, (2) they want comfort, and (3) they want love. Everything a baby needs to survive and be content can be placed in these three categories. Without food, they will die. Without comfort—that is, sleep, peace, safety, and security—they will die either from exhaustion or from the complex chemicals released by anxiety. Without love, they will literally die from lack of contact. The common name for that is *failure to thrive*, and it was documented a few decades ago when infants who weren't picked up or touched enough (for example, orphaned infants in hospitals who were only held for feedings) died from lack of affection and human contact.

As babies grow, they go through a transitory period of goos and blhblihs until they succeed in one-word sentences such as, "Mama." And if you've ever watched that transitory period—the struggle, spitting, gagging, drooling, sputtering, pushing for the sound out of their mouths to match the sound in their ears—you recognize how immensely difficult it is to speak for the first time. Think of the combination of complex muscular movements that must be made in concert to create recognizable words: from the proper exhalation of air in the lungs, the vibration of the vocal cords, and the restriction of air to the sinuses to the movement of the tongue in direct relation to the lips. It's a wonder any of us learn to talk at all.

The question remains: Why do we even bother to learn to speak at all? The baby finally learns to call for "Mama," and everyone around explodes with positive reinforcement. But once the novelty and positive reinforcement of Baby's First Word wear off, what is the advantage of strenuously voicing "Mama" when screaming produced the same result much easier and just as effectively? Or did it?

When Baby says, "Mama," Mama comes. Yet when Baby only

cries, Mama comes, or Dada, or Aunt Laura, or Uncle Doron, or Nana, or smelly cousin Irma. When Baby specifies who Baby wants, Baby gets that person *now*.

When I was in charge of my first niece, Sara, for an afternoon, she cried and reached for something outside her playpen. I brought her the red ball. She screamed. I brought her Mr. Turtle. She screamed. I brought her the blocks, the book, the hat, the keys, the clock: her playpen looked like a garbage heap as the entire room was emptied into her little environment, and she was STILL screaming. Eventually, and I *mean* eventually, I hit on the object she fancied: a large, pink rubber band that was too dangerous for her to have in the first place. As frustrating as it was for me, you can imagine how frustrating it was for her. Speech saves a lot of time, anxiety, and effort. Short sentences—"I want yellow balloon"; "Give me apple juice"; "Pisghetti too hot"—become enormous time/anxiety savers.

As our needs become more specific, advancing from generally needing food to *specifically* needing a pint of Chunky Monkey ice cream, our speech becomes more complex in relation to these needs. Therefore, we can assume: *the complexity of our speech is in direct relation to the complexity of our needs.* And this leads to the prime rule of acting dialogue:

The only reason we ever talk is because we want something we cannot immediately have. There is no exception.

Now, any rule that follows with "there is no exception" means that there must be one, but in years of teaching, I have heard none (save certain neurological conditions, but those are reflexes, not speech).

How about two strangers with nothing in common chatting in a waiting room because their plane is delayed one hour? They don't want anything from each other, will never see each other again, and aren't really interested in the conversation they are having. But they *want* time to pass quicker, and occupying themselves with something like chat makes that seem to happen. They *want* to kill time.

What about when you talk to yourself? The example must be more specific since there are many ways we do this, but each situation follows the rule. Most often we talk to ourselves to sort something out. "Where did I put my . . . ?" or "Why didn't I get that part!?" The voicing of questions helps us focus our mind to answer a dilemma we need solved. That's the literal definition of someone being a "sounding board." The most famous dilemma-solving speech is Hamlet's soliloquy that begins "To be, or not to be."

Perhaps we talk to ourselves to figure something out, like those "easy-assembly" directions. We stare at the page, reading over and over again, until we finally voice, "I already inserted Shelf Five into Bracket Seven. Why doesn't Flange B fit Shelf Five? What IS a 'flange,' anyway?!?!!"

Sometimes we are actually speaking to someone who is not there: "Try THAT again and I'll hand your head to you on a silver platter!" We need to threaten them even if they aren't there to receive it.

Often we *need* to express our deepest feelings to anyone, even if it's the wall. It increases pain to keep them in. Imagine stubbing your toe in the dark, but because your partner is asleep in bed and you don't want to wake him or her, you do *not* shout out "OH [insert expletive-of-your-choosing here]!!!" As you grab your foot and hop around the room like a rabid sea bird, the pain is intensified by the inability to release it. Outward expression of feelings is a basic human need. The same is true of positive feelings and the desire to heighten them through outward expression, such as singing a song or just calling everyone in your address book to say that you got the part. Prayers and ritual songs of celebration have existed since the beginning of our species. Musical theatre relies greatly on the believable truth of releasing heightened emotions to the world whether someone else is there or not: *Carousel*'s "If I Loved You," *West Side Story*'s "I Feel Pretty," *Les Misérable*'s "On My Own," and hundreds of others.

Three Elements to a Formula

Objective

If you have ever said to anyone, "Why are you telling me all this?" it is because you have not been able to perceive any advantage, or need, for them to tell you. Another way of expressing the same concept might be, "What do you want from me?"

People do not talk because they *feel*, they talk because they *want*. When King Lear enters with his beloved daughter Cordelia in his arms, dead by his own deeds, he cries:

> Howl, howl, howl, howl! O, you are men of stones:
> Had I your tongues and eyes, I'd use them so
> That heaven's vault should crack. She's gone forever.

I know when one is dead and when one lives;
She's dead as earth. Lend me a looking-glass;
If that her breath will mist or stain the stone,
Why then she lives.

He does not say this because his most favored daughter is dead and he feels tormented; Cordelia will be dead and he will feel tormented whether he speaks or not. Certainly, he feels all those things and much more, but this is not the reason he speaks.

Lear speaks for a reason: He wants something. Does he want to release his anguish? Does he want to accuse her murderers? Does he want to torture himself? Does he want to bring Cordelia back to life? His reasons do not have to be logical, only *truthful*. How the actor playing Lear chooses to interpret this want can make the difference between a good performance and a brilliant one. But playing the lines for their emotional value without the *need* behind the lines will be hollow, melodramatic, and uninvolving. Skilled script analysis will help you choose your best interpretation. This need—one of the three elements an actor must find to properly analyze a script—is called *the objective* here. Some acting techniques use other words: *motivation*, *want*, *goal*, *intention*, among others. What it is called is far less important than the concept behind it. *The only reason we ever talk is because we want something* [the objective] . . .

Obstacle

. . . *we cannot immediately have.* This leads to the second element of the formula. Examine the logic of this scene:

> DIRECTOR: Can I have your attention, Cast? The second act isn't working. We're going to have to stay late tonight and reblock it. Sorry everyone. Listen, Bill, since you only have that one entrance in the second act, you don't have to stay—you can go.
> BILL *(Drops to knees at DIRECTOR'S feet)*: Please! PLEASE! Let me go tonight! I'm shooting a commercial that's paying my rent this month! Please, I'll do anything, I'll stay late every other night this week! PLEASE PLEASE PLEASE PLEASE!!!

What's wrong with this picture? There is certainly an objective—Bill wants the director to excuse him from rehearsal. But there is no reason to voice these wants because there is nothing he *cannot immediately have*. Because we want to make sense of what is happening, we fill in the blanks. You may have imagined that the actor didn't hear the director, or was too preoccupied, or anticipated the worst and had already prepared a tactic to get out of rehearsal. Since there is recognition of truthful behavior and untruthful behavior, we try to make truthful sense of what we see by guessing the missing pieces.

The missing piece is called *the obstacle* here. The actor determines from the dialogue what is the character's want—the objective—but also what *stands in the way* of that want—the obstacle. Without an obstacle, the objective makes no truthful sense. And this gives us two thirds of our formula for analyzing dialogue. The final third is:

Action

The *action* is what you *play*. You are called an actor. You are not called an emoter, philosopher, feeler, dancer, speaker, thinker, performer, or clown. All of these elements may be an integral part of a good performance, but primarily, before anything else, you must play actions. Even the word *drama* comes from the Greek word for "to do."

Imagine that you are in a fifteen-by-fifteen-foot room with an eight-foot ceiling. The room is primarily built of wood and is enveloped with flames at one end. Fortunately for you, the door is at the other end. What is your objective? Easy enough: You want to get to safety as fast as your legs can carry you. What is the obstacle? Not much except the distance between you and the door, but that's why you have those legs to carry you. Suppose, however, that halfway through, there is a nine-foot-long concrete wall that partly bisected the room. What do you do? Go around it. That's easy. Suppose there is a complete wall, six feet high, made of concrete. (Hint: Remember it's an eight-foot ceiling.) You say you'd climb over it? Very good. Suppose it is wall-to-wall, floor-to-ceiling but made of wallboard—plaster between two layers of paper. Break through it? Good. Suppose now there's a chainlink fence that runs from wall to wall and floor to ceiling. Cut through it? How many rooms have you ever been in with a chainlink-fence cutter on the windowsill? Climb over it? Good try, but it's bolted to the ceiling. But as you begin climbing, you find the bottom is shaky. Sure enough, you pull up the bottom and can climb under it, tearing your linen jacket, but a tear is a lot easier to fix than your ashes.

The objective did not change—you wanted to get out of there with as much flesh as you started. But the obstacle changed, and because the obstacle changed, so did your *action*. And this is the last element of the formula. The three ingredients:

> *Objective:* What the character wants
> *Obstacle:* What stands in the way of the objective
> *Action:* How the character attempts to overcome the obstacle

The formula:

> Objective   +   Obstacle   =   Action

If you know what you want and can identify what stands in your way, then you can choose how best to act on it. Most times the obstacle is unclear, which is why the sequence of actions helps identify the obstacle. For example, although climbing the chainlink fence was futile, it revealed a loose bottom and thus a weakness in the obstacle, and this determined the best action.

This may be how life works most of the time, but scripts work backward. The script is a sequential list of actions. So how can you determine the objective from the end result? The same way people do. Rarely do people come out and say their motivation for doing everything they do. You discern this from what you can *observe* and what you know about them.

Suppose you attend a graduation ceremony where the CEO of a Fortune 500 company is passionately addressing the graduating class. She does it with intensity, love, and conviction. What is her objective? You may conclude that she cares deeply for the emerging generation and wants to impart her wisdom.

But you remember overhearing the CEO say, "Those pretentious, conceited brats can go to hell." Perhaps you then assume she did it for the money. A CEO of a Fortune 500 company? Perhaps not. Perhaps to return a favor to a friend or alma mater. You find out that doesn't apply. Because she was bored that afternoon and had nothing better to do? Because her son is in the graduation class? Because it's a court-mandated, community-service sentence for embezzling funds? All potential solutions. Then, after the speech, she is bestowed an honorary Ph.D. in "recognition of outstanding achievement. . . ." Objectives can become clear quite suddenly through one small action.

And this is why the play cannot be read only once or twice or even *enough*. The script is filled with hundreds of details that can be easily overlooked, but the smallet detail could be the one piece of information crucial to your fully understanding the character or the major ideas within the play.

Look at the opening of John Patrick Shanley's *Danny and the Deep Blue Sea*, a simple love story he calls *an Apache dance*.

> ROBERTA: *31, physically depleted with nervous, bright eyes.*
> DANNY: *29, Chinos and a pullover shirt, dark and powerful.*
> *(Two tables, each illuminated by its own shaded light. ROBERTA sits at one in a vacant sulk, nursing a beer and picking at a bowl of pretzels. Enter DANNY, with a pitcher of beer and a glass. He sits at the other. His hands are badly bruised, and one of his cheeks is cut. He pours himself a beer. A moment passes.)*
>
> DANNY: How 'bout a pretzel?
> ROBERTA: No. They're mine.
> DANNY: You ain't gonna eat all of 'em. Lemme have one.
> ROBERTA: Fuck off.
> DANNY: All right.
> ROBERTA: You wanna pretzel?
> DANNY: Yeah *(Roberta picks up the bowl, takes it to Danny's table, and goes straight back to her seat).*
> ROBERTA: You can have 'em. I'm finished with 'em.
> DANNY: Thanks.
> ROBERTA: You're welcome.
> DANNY: Want some of my beer?
> ROBERTA: No.

Choose an objective for Roberta. Not enough information? Not true. Actually, with some thought and observation, you can deduce a very workable one after the *first two lines*.

Assuming it is a two-character atypically romantic play, you might choose that she is trying to make Danny approach her. But you will find yourself forever rationalizing action after action. Certainly, there is a part of her that is unbearably lonely—perhaps this is why she is in this bar in the first place—but you will have to answer why she denies his request, curses at him, returns to her own table, and rejects his offer. Even though you can justify each of these actions to serve your objective, you will mire her actions in complex mental machinations, and you overlook a consistent objective that is better supported by the words, actions, and overall ideas of the play.

Look again at Shanley's description of Danny when he enters. His hands are *badly bruised* and his cheek is cut. This man is *dark and powerful* and has obviously been in a fight. Roberta, *physically depleted*, is no match for him. Her defiant stance is like a schnauzer threatening a rhinoceros. You might assume that, like a schnauzer, she's too stupid to know better, but this would cheapen her character drastically and diminish the strength of the play. *What does she want?*

Does she want danger? That's a start, but it is not yet an objective. What does she want from *him*? She is deliberately and continually provoking an obviously violent man. "She's looking for someone to crack her head in" might come to mind, but your logic eliminates that as being whacko. But look at what she does. If someone huge and bloody asks you for a pretzel, would you say, "No. They're mine"? If you would answer yes, you must be a lot bigger than me. Or, you want someone to crack your head open.

When you read the rest of the play, you discover Roberta has a self-decreed "unforgivable" sin in her past. She carries this with her always and is repeatedly paying insufficient penance for it. Now, might she want someone to crack her head open? Suddenly, this is no longer "whacko."

Next question: Does she know this? This is a matter of choice. Perhaps she does and believes that if she is maimed or killed she will free herself of her sin. Perhaps she is unconscious of this and believes she is just looking for a night of sex, and only through the potential for violence and the promise of no tenderness can she allow herself to have pleasure. A little research into what an "Apache dance" is could inform that choice. Shanley helps out: *"An Apache Dance is a violent dance for two people, originated by the Parisian apaches—gangsters or ruffians."*

One strong choice: Roberta wants Danny to punish her, the only way she allows herself human contact. The obstacle: Danny has no reason to hurt her, in fact he is terrified of killing someone (again?). Her actions in the scene: to provoke, to taunt, to reject, to challenge, to swear at, and so on.

Analyze the actions of a script the same way you examine the actions of anyone you want to understand. People with profound insight are actually profoundly observant. They study what people do, balanced with what they say, and offer penetrating analysis. It is not an intellectual process; it is an active one.

3 Six Ingredients and Two Spices

"Your talent lies in your choices."
STELLA ADLER

If we could superficially judge performances in three categories, they could be: (1) just plain bad, (2) competent, or (3) brilliant. Although playing a great role can inspire a brilliant performance, any role, if played brilliant*ly*, might accomplish the same result. There is truly no "right" or "wrong" in art—great artists have proven this through centuries of redefinition and expression. However, there is "stronger" and "weaker." The actor who consistently makes strong choices is immeasurably closer to creating a brilliant performance.

In script analysis, there is still no definitively strong or weak choice, but there are stronger or weaker choices for the actor playing the role. Sir Laurence Olivier's choices for Othello are neither stronger nor weaker than James Earl Jones', but for Jones to play Olivier's choices would be weaker *for him*. Nevertheless, there are guidelines that *generally* make strong choices, guidelines that were discovered by Konstantin Stanislavsky, the father of modern acting techniques, and later elaborated on by virtually every actor since then.

The Six Ingredients

A steak is a steak, but *steak au poivre* is magnificent; combine a common steak with sweet cream, aged brandy, and peppercorns, and you create a masterpiece. Add chocolate sauce and mini marshmallows and you have garbage. It's all in the ingredients. When creating the recipe for your character, there are six ingredients and two spices that contribute consistently to the making of strong objectives.

Ingredient Number 1

The objective must be consistent with the words, actions, and circumstances of the script. This is the most obvious choice but the most often overlooked. The script is a list of lines and actions from which you determine an objective. Yet too often an interpretation comes from the *actor's* desire to do or be something on stage rather than from the character's. The Hollywood star–system perpetuates that error the most. The actor playing the part does not want to appear unattractive/mean/unimportant/stupid/unpopular, and so on, so the script is rewritten or simply reinterpreted to be more comfortable to the performer or more positive to his or her career status.

A recent production of Tennessee Williams' *A Streetcar Named Desire* suggested that Blanche wanted Stanley sexually and simply didn't have the courage or want to take responsibility for his making love to her. Even casual study of the play makes it clear that "animal desire," as she calls it, is as abhorrent to her as it is a shameful part of her. It is what has consistently destroyed her life. It causes her to lose her mind at the play's end. And the climactic scene of the play is traditionally referred to as "the rape scene" for reason. Certainly Stanley says, "We've had this date with each other from the beginning," but it is Stanley who says it. Blanche, on the other hand, cries out just prior, "In desperate circumstances. Help me! Caught in a trap!"

Needless to say, the lead in this production was a sexually attractive star, and the advertising poster featured Stanley and Blanche in a passionate embrace. Because the character objectives were inconsistent with the script, the production was weakened.

Ingredient Number 2

The objective must be active. Scenario: You must decide whether to take the lead role in an off-Broadway play or a nonfeatured role in a musical *on* Broadway. The casting directors want your answer in ten minutes. You go home because you do your clearest thinking alone in total silence. Your best friend arrives unexpectedly because she has been offered a promotion, which means more money but much more stress; she needs to discuss this with you.

What is your objective? Let's start with "I want to be alone." As much as Greta Garbo made this famous, it is an unplayable objective. You cannot play a *state of being*. Try doing it right now. Try playing "being alone." Or "being happy." Or "being king." These may be truthful desires, but they cannot be *done*. Stanislavsky said that the actor's job is to translate all feelings and desires into playable *actions*. You may march around the room with a scepter, "off" a few people's "heads," and gorge yourself on roast pig, but these are three actions that the state of "being king" DOES. When confronted with a perceived objective such as "I want to be happy," ask yourself, *"What does 'happy' DO?"*

Ensure that your objective includes an active verb. Take the phrase *"to be"* and eliminate every conjugation of it from your acting vocabulary. (There is *one* exception, which I will discuss in a later chapter.)

Ingredient Number 3
The objective must be phrased in the positive. As long as you're eliminating words from your vocabulary, you may as well take the words NO and NOT and ditch them.

Take the scenario above. Your friend wants—needs—to speak with you about her choice. You could choose as your objective "I don't want to talk to you." The trouble is that this still does not suggest action. Rather, it suggests nonaction. Children play negative actions. It is clear THAT they want, but it is unclear even to themselves WHAT they want. They know they "want to do something fun." So you, as a good little uncle, suggest something.

"Would you like to go to a movie?"

"Naw."

"Would you like to get a hamburger?"

"No."

"How about the beach?"

"No."

"Play a game?"

"No."

"Get ice cream?"

"No."

"Go outside?"

"No."

"Stay inside?"

"No."

(*Lock you in a closet 'til you pass out. . . ?*)

Playing a negative is not only undoable, it's annoying. Watching the men's champion tennis player competing against the women's champion tennis player could be thrilling (regardless of any bias you may have as to the "inevitable" winner), but watching either one of those experts playing against a garage door is not nearly as engaging. If you did watch, would you be more interested in the player or the garage door? The garage door can only say, "No." The ball can be hit by the player in hundreds of directions, styles, and powers; the garage door can only say, "No." Don't diminish your characters into garage doors.

Fortunately, the world is created from opposites: every night has a day; every male has a female; every Yin has a Yang; and every positive has a negative. Change the child's objective from "I don't want to do *that* (movie, hamburger, game, outside, inside)" to "I *do* want you to entertain me with something fun." Change "I don't want to talk to you" to "I *do* want to figure out my problem." But this still isn't strong enough.

Ingredient Number 4

The objective must involve your partner. "I want to figure out my problem" is both active and phrased in the positive, but it is isolated from your partner. Theatre relies on the back-and-forth interaction between performers so that the audience can vicariously slip in. Completely self-involved actions are not interesting to watch. How long can you "watch" someone read? But if they are reading *for you*, you are engaged. This "for you" is crucial to effective theatre. During the 1960s, popular dancing was an isolated activity. If you were within two feet of your partner, you were too close. People's arms waved wildly and feet flailed, it didn't matter if your eyes were open or closed, and the necessity for a dance *partner* was debatable. As athletically fun as this may have been to do, it was relatively boring to watch. Soon partnered disco dancing dominated, and although it may have been a questionable art, it was engaging enough to inspire a major film and its sequel (*Saturday Night Fever*). I can't recall there being a film called *The Funky Chicken*. Watching a solitaire game is dull; watching a poker game is interesting. Watching someone eat is dull; watching someone feed a baby is interesting. And messy.

The "partner" in a play can be anyone on stage with you, someone your character *believes* is onstage with you, the audience, or yourself. The partner in Hamlet's soliloquy ("To be, or not to be") might be a conflicting side of himself, or God, or his father. The partner in *Medea* is the Greek Chorus. Tom's partner in *The Glass Menagerie* is the audience, and they can represent the world, his conscience, fellow merchant marines, or truly anyone you, as the actor playing him, want them to be.

If we change from the previous scenario, "I want to figure out my problem" to "I want you to leave me alone," we have a lot more to do in our scene.

Many acting techniques use a "private moment" exercise. Of the various purposes it serves, primarily it is meant to train actors out of self-consciousness and teach them to behave truthfully in front of an audience. Although valid, it is not theatre. If the exercise takes place in a class, then you are engaged in the challenge of a classmate's struggle to complete a task effectively. But if watching people behave naturally and only for themselves were theatre, then public restrooms would sell admission tickets.

Ingredient Number 5

The objective must include conflict. Ideally, *the conflict is how you perceive your partner's objective.* Conflict is the oxygen of drama; without conflict, there is only discussion and activity. Your objective cannot thrive without an obstacle. If your best friend from our scenario discovers your dilemma and says immediately, "Oh my, you only have ten minutes to decide! Should I leave you alone?" then we have a short, boring scene.

If you choose your objective with the condition, "*I want* _____ *BUT you want* _____ *(and we both can't win)*," then you are well on your way to intriguing drama. For our scenario, "I want you to leave me alone, but you want me to solve your career problem" becomes interactive and conflicting.

Be wary that you don't allow your characters to know more than they do. Remember: *Your character has not read the play.* A PERCEIVED conflict is as playable as a genuine one. In Thornton

Wilder's *Our Town*, there is a charming scene that takes place in Mr. Morgan's soda shop. George wants Emily to be his girlfriend. Emily wants George to be her boyfriend. So far, there is no conflict. But the scene works extremely well because George and Emily do not know how the other feels. The mistake would be to decide that the obstacle is their own nervousness, because this would eliminate the strongest interaction between the characters. Remember, the obstacle is *outside of yourself.*

The key lies in a previous scene, when Emily confronts George on his childishness, self-involvement, conceit, and preoccupation with baseball. George wants Emily to be his girlfriend, BUT he perceives that Emily thinks him self-centered, stuck-up, and immature. Sure enough, in the soda shop scene, he woos her with generosity, expressing interest in her ideas and concerns, demonstrating care for the people around him, and taking to heart her "honest appraisals." These actions are designed to overcome the perceived obstacle of her negative opinion of him. Emily, on the other hand, remembers what she said and also knows that outspoken, overly critical girls—in 1901 when the play is set—are less attractive and eventually pull their hair back tight and work in the library 'til they die alone. So she courts him with agreement, drinking in his every word, acquiescing to his wisdom, and encouraging and supporting his decisions. All these actions are designed to overcome the perception that he believes her to be aggressively fault-finding. The audience knows the truth but is engaged in the characters' *process* because we know that they don't have our knowledge.

Ingredient Number 6

The objective must arouse you artistically. This one is a lot easier said than done. After analyzing a script, you may find an objective that is quite apparent to you. In fact the character may come right out and say it. But it is not an objective you can get excited about. Perhaps you don't agree with it philosophically or morally, or what the character finds of crucial importance, you find frivolous and mundane. Your choice might be to change the objective to something that better suits your frame of mind. This would be a critical mistake. For the same reasons that you do not choose objectives that are contrary to the script's actions and words, you cannot bend an objective to be more accessible to you. You must bring yourself to the script, not bring the script to you.

In the early second century B.C., the Roman and first-known black playwright, Terence, said, "I am a man: nothing human is alien to me." He was talking about compassion and the universality of all human experience. Everyone's individual life experiences are limited, but our ability to feel compassion is limit*less*, and for this reason—with imagination and hard work—we can relate to any character's objective.

In Terrence McNally's *The Lisbon Traviata*, Mendy is desperate for a copy of Maria Callas' performance of the play's title. His objective might be quite apparent to you, but perhaps you don't care for opera or cannot relate to an urgent need to hear a particular piece of music. Ask yourself if you've ever been desperate for any *thing*. Have you ever left your house at 2:00 in the morning for a pint of Fudge Brownie Overload? Called someone's answering machine *just* to hear his or her voice? This is when your compassion can create a parallel that you can relate to, and you can say, "Ah! That's how Mendy must feel about Callas' *Lisbon Traviata*."

Perhaps you are one of those lucky people who has never seriously considered suicide. How do you play Hamlet's famous soliloquy ("To be, or not to be . . .") if that's what you interpret he is doing? Or Babe's last assent up the stairs in Beth Henley's *Crimes of the Heart*? You must be willing to delve into your own dark side in order to find your compassionate link. Exactly what is suicide? Is it a coward's escape? Or is it an end to pain, to (as Hamlet relates) "the heart-ache and the thousand natural shocks that flesh is heir to"? Ask yourself and try to recall what the greatest pain you ever experienced was, whether it was physical, emotional, or spiritual. Use any technique you can to remember that dark period of your life. Ask yourself how your fight would have changed if you knew that this pain would never end—if you believed to the point of factual knowledge that this pain would blanket the rest of your life, that peace or even a smile would never be natural to your days. If this were true, might you consider putting an end to it with the only option available? If your pain was physical, can you now relate to similar wishes in agony-ridden, terminal cancer victims? If the pain was emotional, do you begin to understand the exhausting burdens of Hamlet and Babe?

The objective you choose may fulfill the first five criteria and even be something you fully *understand*, but if that connection is purely intellectual, it will never couple with your artistry. What every actor must do is "pay the price." This means that whatever the character goes through, you must create it fully—and sometimes this is quite personally costly.

In the film *Sophie's Choice*, Meryl Streep gives a brilliant performance of the climactic scene. This moment of the title character's choice is phenomenally powerful and the audience sits forward, mouth agape, with adrenaline-induced anxiety. But what level did Ms. Streep have to experience in order to create that level of experience in her audience? Greatness is costly. The great joy of acting is that you can experience these things, grow from the experience, create the truth, and find they leave no scars. Because they are only as real as your worst nightmare. Or deepest fantasy. The stage is the safest place on earth where we know virtually everything in advance and can be certain we will be able to smile at our curtain call. We can rule the world, murder our children, conquer the South Pole, blind ourselves, or die, and still go out afterward for pizza. Acting is a roller coaster that makes you fear for your life or live a thrilling free fall. But experienced only intellectually, it becomes a detailed documentary about roller coaster riding. Which would you rather do?

Beginning your objective with "I want you to _____" and inserting an active verb in the blank will help you incorporate the six ingredients:

1. It must be consistent with the play's words and actions.
2. It must be active.
3. It must be phrased in the positive.
4. It must involve your partner.
5. It must have an obstacle (ideally, your character's perception of your partner's objective).
6. It must arouse you artistically.

Most objectives will not be as difficult as debating your choice to live or die, but with compassion, suspension of self-image and personal opinions, and intelligent insight, you can arouse yourself to any objective.

The Two Spices

Spice Number One: Stakes
Defining question: What do I have to gain or lose, should my character achieve or not achieve his or her objective?

Do you like to be on time? (I hope so, because lateness is a good way to miss your audition slot or get fired from a show during that two-week "window.") Imagine you are leaving the house for work and you see an Overnight Express truck parked exactly halfway on a one-dollar bill. Would you try to pull it out? Maybe, but don't bother; it's stuck under there. Would you wait for the truck to leave? That depends on your financial status. (It could mean the difference between walking to work and riding a bus.) How long would you wait? After all, how long does an Overnight Express truck stay in one place—isn't that their point? Let's say you might wait a few seconds. If you then don't see the driver nearby, you might leave.

How about a five-dollar bill? A bit longer? Maybe a minute or two, time to read the headlines at the newsstand the truck is in front of.

A ten-dollar bill? A few minutes more. Maybe five minutes? You could make up an excuse to your boss for ten bucks.

A twenty. Maybe a bit longer. Six, seven, ten minutes? Depending on your hourly wage, you can afford to get docked an hour for twenty bucks tax-free.

A fifty-dollar bill? Now we're getting serious. Maybe fifteen minutes to a half hour?

How about a genuine, Benjamin Franklin, United States of America one-hundred-dollar bill? Some might wait an hour, some might be willing to call in sick for the day. Some people might even welcome the excuse to quit their jobs for a hundred bucks free and clear.

Suppose that the truck is parked exactly halfway and immovably on your state's lottery ticket. You look at the date and number on the ticket and compare it to the date and number posted at that newsstand and see that they match. Number for number. How long would you wait? In my state, the lowest winning is about a million dollars, and I don't know about you, but for a million bucks I'd camp out by the truck and go hungry for a week or three 'til the stupid thing moved. I'd be able to afford the hospital bills.

In all instances, the objective remains the same: to take free money. The subsequent actions, or more precisely, the intensity of those actions, becomes stronger because the stakes are higher. The higher the stakes, the harder you work. What are the odds of winning a lottery if you played it? Five million to one? But people play the lottery regularly because the stakes are so irresistibly high.

In Edmond Rostand's *Cyrano de Bergerac*, the title character wants his cousin Roxanne to fall in love with him (back then, those things were kosher). The stakes implied for winning the heart of someone you love are universal. The fact that he has been in love with her since they were children makes them higher. The fact that she is falling in love with someone else heightens them even more. As the play spans its decades, his faithful commitment to her builds the emotional stakes as high as possible; he has devoted his entire life to her.

There is also the reverse question: What do I have to lose? Many years ago, *Sixty Minutes* aired an episode about the danger of trailer-home design. In those days, the windows were very small— usually jalousies (louvered glass slats)—and there was generally one door. In one trailer home, a fire broke out in the hallway between the bedroom and the only door. A man was trapped in that bed-room. The camera showed the trailer after the fire, and when it zoomed in on a bedroom wall, it revealed fingernail scratches. The trapped man's tragic objective was obvious, but what were the odds that he would scratch his way out, find a weakness in the alu-minum, exhibit superhuman strength, or be the recipient of a mira-cle? Five-zillion to one? Nevertheless, he strove; the stakes were the highest anyone can have: life or death.

Larry Kramer's *The Normal Heart* is about a writer during the beginnings of AIDS. A doctor begs him to inform the gay culture of the dangers of promiscuous sex. The writer knows the unpopularity of this stance, but also witnesses friends dying. As more people die, the stakes get higher. As his first and only lover begins dying and the government continues to ignore the facts, the stakes heighten. Although it is never mentioned in the play, the actor playing the writer knows that he himself potentially carries the disease; his own life is at stake, too.

"Life" can be defined also as "life as I know it." Someone wholly devoted to a job might find it "life or death" should he or she be at risk of losing it. A child, a marriage, a dear friend, a home, eyesight, self-sufficiency, speech, freedom—all of these can define "life as you know it," and the potential loss of them can be equivalently life-threatening. Ken Harrison, the major character in Brian Clark's *Whose Life Is It, Anyway?*, fights to commit suicide because he loses the use of his hands. Ken Harrison is a sculptor.

The playwright does not always reveal high stakes within the script. Often in comedies realistically tangible high stakes can be distracting from the comedic point of view. Nevertheless, for comedy to work, your performance must be heightened, perhaps to nearly absurdism, without sacrificing truth. You must give yourself stakes in order to justify your performance size.

In *Harvey*, by Mary Chase, Elwood P. Dowd's sister Veta-Louise wants to commit her brother to a psychiatric hospital because he spends all his time and converses with Harvey, a six-foot white rabbit whom nobody—including the audience—seems to see. Chase shows us the embarrassment it is to Veta-Louise, especially during a time when she is trying to marry off her daughter, but this may not be enough justification for you to warrant the character's injection of her brother with experimental psychiatric drugs simply to save her embarrassment. This is where that all-important imagination comes in. Suppose you've read articles that serial killers begin by speaking to mythical beasts (like "son of Sam") and they start by murdering siblings. Suppose you yourself have begun seeing Harvey during those late nights before sleep and fear for your own sanity. Suppose you had a pet rabbit as a child who always bit your finger and you live in terror that Harvey is going to bite off your face. Whatever gets your blood rushing can be used as your character's stakes—the audience need never know.

If you can elevate your character's stakes to life or death, then your scenes will never be boringly casual or low energy.

Spice Number Two: Urgency
Defining question: Why now?

There is a marvelously theatrical scene in the beginning of Fannie Flagg's screenplay for *Fried Green Tomatoes*. The main character, a girl of about eight, has a big brother who is established right away as an instantly lovable and charming young man. While crossing a bridge, her new hat blows off her head and lands in the railroad tracks below. He chivalrously tromps down the embankment to retrieve it for her. He keeps grabbing for it, yet it keeps blowing away. He finally lunges and snatches it, but his foot gets caught in a rail switch. Waving calmly to his sister and the group watching on the bridge, he wriggles his foot to extricate himself. The Depression-era family cannot afford the financial sacrifice of the boot. Then, over the treetops, the observers see puffs of smoke. They call to him as he struggles harder to release the shoe. The train whistle is heard, he abandons saving the boot, and hurriedly begins unlacing the many rows. The train appears and he frantically tears at the laces. The closer the train gets, the more frenzied his struggle becomes.

From the moment the brother's foot is entrapped, his life is at stake; that doesn't change. What does change is *time*. The scene would be far less theatrical if the crowd were yelling, "Hurry! There's a train coming!! IN TWO HOURS!!!" The closer the train comes, the more *urgent* is his objective. If you've ever been surfing through the several thousand cable channels looking for something to watch, and you see someone climbing a sheer cliff with a rope, and you then see that the strands of the rope are beginning to snap, don't you hesitate your surf for the few minutes it takes to see whether the climber makes it before the rope snaps? The stakes, again, are the same, but the more strands that pop, the more urgent it becomes that the climber achieve that objective *now*.

Michael Cristoffer's *The Shadow Box* is about three families who struggle to resolve past conflicts. Why must they resolve these problems now? The interwoven plots take place in a hospice for terminal cancer patients; the urgency is obvious. In *A Doll House*, by Henrik Ibsen, Nora wants to forestall an inevitable disclosure made tangible by a letter waiting in the locked mailbox. As time speeds by, her frantic attempts to distract her husband build until she literally dances herself into frenzied exhaustion.

As with stakes, often the urgency must be imagined to give your performance life. Sometimes the urgency simply becomes "I cannot stand it a moment longer." This emotional urgency fuels Martha's confession in *The Children's Hour*, Tom's attacks in *The Glass Menagerie*, and Romeo's trespass into the Capulet garden just to catch a glimpse of his beloved. Oftentimes before taking an exit in a weak play, I have imagined taxicab meters ticking downstairs. As with stakes, if your imagination helps boil your blood, it can only help the scene.

The higher the stakes and the more urgent the circumstances, the harder you try. The harder you try, the more intense are your actions. The more intense your actions, the more captivating your performance.

◢ꓯ Bit by Beat

Accomplishing the objective of any large task is chaotic if approached from its entirety rather than taken step by step. After throwing a wild party, one look at what's left of your home can be overwhelming. But when you first tackle the dishes, then those mysterious stains in the rug, then the guest sleeping in the coat closet, you focus on the individual tasks that lead to restoring your home rather than remain overpowered by the entire chore's magnitude. You focus on process instead of result.

Those "process steps" in a script are *beats*. In Stanislavsky, they are also translated as *units*. (When Richard Boleslavsky was lecturing on Stanislavsky's techniques, he used the word *bits*, but with his strong Russian accent, the students wrote down *beats*, which is why in America we have adopted this term.) The beats within a scene are composed of the actions which, step by step, strive to accomplish that objective.

Stanislavsky analogizes the breakdown of a scene into beats with eating a turkey. When eating a turkey, your objective is to get the nourishment of that bird into your bloodstream. However, if you move directly to the *result* of that objective instead of breaking it down to the component parts necessary to *achieve* it, you would have to swallow that turkey whole, or inject it directly into your bloodstream—both of which would foster some hideously prohibitive medical bills. But if you *break it down* to the necessary steps that accomplish this result, you develop a sequence of actions leading to success.

First you break off a drumstick thus dividing the turkey into smaller parts. Then you cut off a "bite-sized" morsel defined only by the capacity of your mouth. You don't swallow that bite unless you're a German shepherd; you chew it into smaller bits. After swallowing, your stomach acids break it down even into smaller bits. The digestion process continues until the turkey is broken down to microscopic parts that can be absorbed by your digestive tract.

The laws of nature—and scripts—follow complex sequences of actions to accomplish their objectives.

Beats and Rhythm

In script analysis, what it all comes down to again is action: what the character *does* to achieve his or her objective. If you are to animate the incomplete words of the script, it must be through actions. *Animate* comes from the Latin word *animare*, which means "to fill with breath." An inanimate object is not alive.

The more varied your actions, the more interesting your performance will be as you bring the play to life. Whether the artist creates with pigments, actions, shapes, movements, sounds, textures, ideas, words, lights, rhythms, or anything tangible, the variety of elements precipitate the richness of the work. An actor without actions is like a painter without paints.

Even the strongest, most exciting action has a shelf life. Nothing, absolutely nothing, is interesting without change. A great dancer may be able to leap seemingly miles off the ground, but you would not want to watch hour after hour of those leaps in repetition. Can you imagine a full-length opera of only one, magnificent high note? A work of visual art remains interesting because there are always new ways to see it. Wallpaper is not interesting because it is intentionally repetitious. Scripts have little need for actor wallpaper. In film, they're called "extras."

Conversely, be wary that you do not change actions so often that none of them have any "teeth." Too many actions fleeting by the audience appear chaotic and unfocused. Think of a buffet smorgasbord: You wouldn't choose only one food no matter how delicious;

otherwise, there's no point in the buffet. And you also wouldn't take equal amounts of everything there. One egg roll, one strand of spaghetti, one roast. You vary each food according to its interest to you. Four oysters, a heap of spaghetti, one caviar cracker. The greater the variety—not only in tastes but in quantities—the more satisfying your plate.

Once you choose an objective for your character, begin to identify the strongest actions suggested by the script that accomplish that goal and overcome the perceived obstacle. The duration of that action *defines* the duration of a beat. When the action changes, a new beat begins.

As long as the beat continues, the action defining it must *build*. If it doesn't, it is only repetition—wallpaper. *Build* does not necessarily mean in vocal volume, but in intensity. This intensity can be expressed through volume, rhythm, emotional intensity, or infinite ways that an action can turn up the wattage as stakes become higher and more urgent. The quicker the change in action, the faster the pace of the scene.

So the breakdown of a scene is like driving a car. One continuous action with steady build is like driving hours on a Nevada highway. Too many actions without opportunity to build is like crossing Manhattan at rush hour. But if your scene has twists and turns, hills and cliffs, and periodic stretches that allow you to really burn rubber, no one's attention will wander.

The nature of the script determines the rhythm of the scene. A fight has relatively fast and intense beats. A debate has longer, intellectually paced cadences. A love scene can slowly blossom with romance, burst suddenly with violent passion, or simmer slowly until it savagely explodes. Comedy and tragedy have their timing and pace. Verse commands forward momentum. But regardless of the ultimate rhythms chosen, they are governed by the action changes and builds within the beats.

Defining Beats

Examine the beginning of a scene from Clifford Odets' *Waiting for Lefty*.

This confrontation has high stakes and urgency as well as the opportunity for a great variety of beats and rhythms. The play takes place in 1931 before unions were strong or effective. The country was steeped in the Depression, and labor was being abused with slavish hours and arbitrary pay cuts. In the following scene Joe, a hardworking cabdriver in New York City, comes home to a house emptied of all furnishings. Edna, his wife, has been watching their children waste away from malnutrition and illness. She sees clearly the critical necessity for some kind of revolution. She knows that a labor strike is the only way to force management to change. Here are the conflicting objectives: She wants Joe to fight for his family but Joe, unwilling to face harsh reality, wants her to support his passive leadership.

(Joe comes in, home from work. For a moment they stand and look at each other in silence.)

JOE: Where's all the furniture, honey?

EDNA: They took it away. No installments paid.

JOE: When?

EDNA: Three o'clock.

JOE: They can't do that.

EDNA: Can't? They did it.

JOE: Why, the palookas, we paid three-quarters.

EDNA: The man said read the contract.

JOE: We must have signed a phony . . .

EDNA: It's a regular contract and you signed it.

JOE: Don't be so sour, Edna . . . *(Tries to embrace her.)*

EDNA: Do it in the movies, Joe—they pay Clark Gable big money for it.

JOE: This is a helluva house to come home to. Take my word!

EDNA: Take MY word! Whose fault is it?

JOE: Must you start that stuff again?

EDNA: Maybe you'd like to talk about books?

JOE: I'd like to slap you in the mouth!

EDNA: No you won't.

JOE *(Sheepishly)*: Jeez, Edna, you get me sore some time. . . .

EDNA: But just look at me—I'm laughing all over!

JOE: Don't insult me. Can I help it if times are bad? What the hell do you want me to do, jump off a bridge or something?

EDNA: Don't yell. I just put the kids to bed so they won't know they missed a meal. If I don't have Emmy's shoes soled tomorrow, she can't go to school. In the meantime, let her sleep.

Obviously, this is an argument. A weak choice would be to begin the scene with casual intensity in order to give yourself room to build. But that eliminates the script's note that Edna has been stewing since three o'clock. She also had to solve the problem of how to keep young children occupied enough to forget they had no dinner before going to bed. To choose that the scene starts quietly weakens our belief in her high stakes and urgency.

The scene starts strong and gets stronger. Played well, it is enormously powerful. This play caused a riot of labor support from the audience on opening night; this wasn't because of its low-key subtlety.

Next, those strong actions must vary; otherwise the scene will be reduced to a screaming match. Let's start choosing them. If you begin with Joe's opening line, you are missing important preparation. Odets writes, *"For a moment, they stand and look at each other."* But what does that mean? Is that all they do? If you came home and found that the car you let your brother borrow was now smashed, would you "look at" your brother when he came home? Or would you *kill* him with your glare? The cliché "if looks could kill" describes a specific action that is strong and playable.

Once again, it is imperative to note that the actions delineated here are not "definitive" actions for this scene; there is no "right" or "wrong" in art, only stronger and weaker. They comprise ONE set of choices that would be strong and supported by the script.

1st Action: Edna *attacks* Joe.

Joe, on the other hand, is expecting to come home after an exhausting ten-hour workday to a loving wife and adoring children in a furnished apartment. He is confronted with bare floors and a wife who is attacking him with her eyes. He needs to know what's going on.

2nd Action: Joe *gropes* for answers.

This first beat lasts as long as those two actions are continued. How long does the beat last?

> JOE: Where's all the furniture, honey?
> EDNA: They took it away. No installments paid.
> JOE: When?
> EDNA: Three o'clock.
> [then]
> JOE: They can't do that.

Is he still groping for answers? Or does he understand what happened, and why Edna is furious?

3rd Action: Joe *blames* the furniture people. What better way to prove your innocence than by shifting the guilt?

> EDNA: Can't? They did it.

Does Edna still attack? Perhaps so. But since Joe's action changes, the beat changes nevertheless because anything that happens on stage is a collaboration between partners. For the actor playing Edna, the intensity of her attack will build.

> JOE: Why, the palookas, we paid three-quarters.
> EDNA: The man said read the contract.

Refusing to let Joe pass the buck, she *condemns* him for making such a stupid error. The next two lines build within the same beat as Joe still *blames*.

> JOE: We must have signed a phony . . .
> EDNA: It's a regular contract and you signed it.
> [until]
> JOE: Don't be so sour, Edna . . . (*Tries to embrace her.*)

This could be a *command* for Joe. But Odets' stage direction suggests he is *comforting* her. *Soothing* her. *Cheering her up.* The choices are numerous and you will ONLY know the best choice for you by TRYING it.

> EDNA: Do it in the movies, Joe—they pay Clark Gable big money
>   for it.

She *rejects* him.

> JOE: This is a hellava house to come home to. Take my word!

The best defense is an offense, so he *attacks* back. Her job as a 1931 housewife is to make a comfortable, loving home.

> EDNA: Take MY word! Whose fault is it?

She *blames* him.

> JOE: Must you start that stuff again?

Fatigued, he *appeals* to her sympathies.

EDNA: Maybe you'd like to talk about books?

As rich as the English language is, it still lacks some words to express specific actions. Sometimes they need to be invented. Being sarcastic is a common, specific (albeit low) way to make your point. My suggestion: she *sarcasticizes*.

JOE: I'd like to slap you in the mouth!

He *threatens*.

EDNA: No you won't.

She *challenges*.

JOE: Jeez, Edna, you get me sore sometime. . . .

He *apologizes*.

EDNA: But just look at me—I'm laughing all over!

She *parades* her exasperation.

JOE: Don't insult me.

He *scolds* her.

Can I help it if times are bad?

He *accuses* society.

What the hell do you want me to do, jump off a bridge or
   something?

He *ridicules* her for blaming him when it is not his fault. Your actions can change midsentence if the script supports it.

EDNA: Don't yell. I just put the kids to bed so they won't know
   they missed a meal. If I don't have Emmy's shoes soled
   tomorrow, she can't go to school.

Their children are going to bed hungry and at risk of being denied an education; she *condemns* him.

In the meantime, let her sleep.

Her condemnation builds until it evolves into a *command*.

If you were now to map out this scene breakdown into its beats, it would be:

	EDNA	VS.	JOE
1ST BEAT:	<u>Attack</u>	vs.	Grope
2ND BEAT:	Attack	vs.	<u>Blame</u>
3RD BEAT:	<u>Condemn</u>	vs.	Blame
4TH BEAT:	Reject	vs.	<u>Cheer up</u>
5TH BEAT:	Blame	vs.	<u>Attack</u>
6TH BEAT:	Sarcasticize	vs.	<u>Appeal</u>
7TH BEAT:	Challenge	vs.	<u>Threaten</u>
8TH BEAT:	Parade	vs.	<u>Apologize</u>
9TH BEAT:	Ridicule	vs.	<u>Accuse</u>

The underlined actions are those that initiate the beat change.

Few scenes will suggest beat changes as rapidly as this, and it becomes chaotic to change on every line, but in this example, the scene begins with constant jabs because the urgency and stakes are so high that they support this choice. It's like a fistfight with quick footwork, sudden reverses, and surprise attacks. The rapid succession of punches in this scene contribute to its fierce pace until the characters center on the real problem and Edna zeroes in on the strongest actions to overcome her obstacle. At that point, the beats become longer as the chosen actions build with heated intensity.

However, there are hundreds of alternative interpretations equally effective. One would be to begin with fewer actions and longer beats that build higher. For example:

	EDNA		JOE
1ST BEAT:	<u>Accuse</u>	vs.	Defend

JOE: Where's all the furniture, honey?
EDNA: They took it away. No installments paid.
JOE: When?
EDNA: Three o'clock.

JOE: They can't do that.
EDNA: Can't? They did it.
JOE: Why, the palookas, we paid three-quarters.
EDNA: The man said read the contract.
JOE: We must have signed a phony . . .
EDNA: It was a regular contract and you signed it.

2ND BEAT: Reject	vs.	<u>Appeal</u> (to her sympathies)

JOE: Don't be so sour, Edna. . . . *(Tries to embrace her.)*
EDNA: Do it in the movies, Joe—they pay Clark Gable big money for it.
JOE: This is a hellava house to come home to. Take my word!
EDNA: Take MY word! Whose fault is it?
JOE: Must you start that stuff again?
EDNA: Maybe you'd like to talk about books?

3RD BEAT: Challenge	vs.	<u>Threaten</u>

JOE: I'd like to slap you in the mouth!
EDNA: No you won't.

4TH BEAT: Protest	vs.	<u>Defend</u>

JOE *(Sheepishly)*: Jeez, Edna, you get me sore some time. . . .
EDNA: But just look at me—I'm laughing all over!
JOE: Don't insult me. Can I help it if times are bad? What the hell do you want me to do, jump off a bridge or something?
EDNA: Don't yell. I just put the kids to bed so they won't know they missed a meal. If I don't have Emmy's shoes soled tomorrow, she can't go to school. In the meantime, let her sleep.

Which is better? No such thing. Depending on the actors, director, and year of its production, the strongest choices are those that bring the script to life and command an audience's involvement. How do you decide *which* is best for you? There's only one way: *Try them.*

Strong Versus Weak

As you break down a scene into beats, you must specify the actions that define them. Without specification, you are dangerously close to "winging it" with a vague, inconsistent performance. The actor's script breakdown is the personal blueprint from which you have constructed your performance. The script is the architectural design; your breakdown is the construction materials sheet. By their nature, some actions are more interesting than others.

A STRONG action is:	A WEAK action is:
1. Expressed as an active verb.	1. Passive.
2. Specific.	2. Vague.
3. Exciting to watch.	3. Ordinary.
4. Directed at your partner.	4. Internally focused.
5. Personally involving.	5. Distant from you.
6. Able to be physicalized.	6. Static/stagnant.

"To chat" is one of the least interesting actions, but it is often used by actors who assume that being "natural" is equivalent to being interesting. Remember, if "natural" were theatre, public restrooms would sell tickets.

Take, for example, this speech from the end of the scene we've examined in Chapter 4 from *Waiting for Lefty*. Edna must convince Joe to rally his friends for a strike.

> JOE: One man can't—[make a strike]
> EDNA: I don't say one man. I say a hundred, a thousand, a whole
> million, I say. But start in your own union. Get those hack
> boys together. Sweep out those racketeers like a pile of dirt.
> Stand up like men and fight for the crying kids and wives.

Action choices for this beat, from weaker to stronger, include:

To *tell*: Weak. Too common and stagnant.

To *inform*: Better. At least it's less prosaic.

To *enlighten*: Better still. It now involves the partner more strongly, but it is primarily an intellectual result.

To *inspire*: Even stronger. This suggests physical movement. The nature of this action opposes sitting back in a chair and talking casually.

To *electrify*: Very strong. Not only does it command "physical-ization," involve her partner, and specify an uncommon action, but it is alive and exciting to watch—the actor's ultimate goal.

A virtually useless choice for this speech would be to *promulgate*. Even if you knew the definition, this is a word that a fraction of ac-tors would find personal: "I think I'll call up Mom and promulgate my idea." If you are one of the rare birds who think this way, by all means, use it. But an action chosen only intellectually is as un-playable as an objective chosen that way.

Reread the speech, imagining each of those actions. Better yet, *play* the speech out loud, *doing* each of those actions.

Every action has its "nature," and its nature has: (1) tone, (2) rhythm, and (3) physicality. The nature of to *soothe* is not superfast at the top of your lungs while darting around the room. And the na-ture of to *panic* is not whispery and slow while propping your feet on the coffee table.

Using a thesaurus to build your action vocabulary can be as hindering as it is helpful. The *skill* you must learn is how to *think* in terms of actions. If you rely on an external source to find it for you, you cannot build that skill and you severely limit your spontaneity as well as your creativity. Take a look at this speech from Edward Albee's *Who's Afraid of Virginia Woolf?*:

> GEORGE: It's perfectly all right for you . . . I mean, you can make your own rules . . . you can go around like a hopped-up Arab, slashing away at everything in sight, scarring up half the world if you want to. But somebody else try it . . . no sir!

If you play George, you may choose to *insult* your partner. But you may also find yourself playing that action too often to maintain interest. So you run to your thesaurus for shades of the same color and find: to *belittle*, to *slander*, or to *revile*. But if you connect with the scene and are skilled at thinking in actions, you may come up with choices that are not literal alternatives but are personal or metaphoric ones: to *pulverize*, to *slap around*, to *crucify*.

Choosing actions is not a word game that tests vocabulary. It is a technique to *specify* an action tangibly by using a word. The word you choose then specifies the tone, rhythm, and physicality of that action.

More Actions to Avoid

Boring Actions

Watching a trapeze artist is exciting except to another trapeze artist; actions that fill the bulk of our daily lives are boring to watch someone else do. People do not go to the theatre to see the ordinary. How interesting are other people's "home movies"? Talk is one of the most common and ordinary actions that fill our days. Very, very few performers can make talk interesting. To *tell*, to *ask*, to *talk*, to *explain*, and to *chat* are too common and—worse—are only about words. The playwright gives you the words but prays that you fill them with unique and intriguing action.

Intellectual Processes

Actions that occur in the mind are illegible to an audience. To *respect* is not an action; it is an invisible frame of mind. To *understand*, to *consider*, to *appreciate* are all intellectual processes. When the script suggests *respect* to you, translate it with an additional question: What does respect DO? Respect can *admire*, *worship*, *bow to*, *welcome*, *submit*, and *honor*. Similarly, appreciation can *thank*, *applaud*, *praise*, *agree*, *support*, and *salute*.

- Exception 1: When your partner has "a moment" that should command primary importance, instead of merely *hearing*, you can choose an intellectual action to remain alive without distracting from the scene's focus. Get ready to ditch it once you begin your next line.
- Exception 2: In filmed work, specifically in a close-up, the camera is so near and intimate that the processes of the mind can be communicated effectively. This is because the subtle physicalizations of thought that are too small for stage are registered by the magnified image. During intense thought, the eyes glimmer, the brows make small movements, or the jaw tenses. Also, the nature of a close-up excludes the scene partner for a brief period of time, so internal actions work. Film scripts are written with images, and an expressive face can communicate a great deal of ideas better than words.

Emotional Actions

Any action that describes a feeling—to *love*, to *envy*, to *worry*, to *enjoy*, to *get upset*, to *anguish*, to *hate*—are not playable. One of the great frustrations of human relationships is that it is impossible for you to see what another person thinks or feels. Neither can an audience. Treat these like intellectual actions. Ask yourself, What does hate DO? Hate *attacks*, *insults*, *dismisses*, *ridicules*, *rejects*, or *incriminates*. It is from these actions that the watcher perceives that emotional state.

Evaluations and Judgments

Actions examined collectively or altered by information are evaluations and judgments of actions. For example, if your friend *coerces* you to spend a day on his boat, *commands* you as his crew, and *patronizes* you with his superior knowledge, you would evaluate his collective actions as trying to *control* you. But his actions are *coerce*, *command*, and *patronize*. If a friend *invites* you to go out, *teases* you about spending too much time inside, and *begs* you for your companionship, and then you discover upon returning that there is a surprise party waiting for you, you may realize that your friend *manipulated* you out of the house. The three actions judged with the information that there was a party allowed you to recognize it as manipulation. But the action was not to manipulate; the actions were to *invite*, *tease*, and *beg*. Too many actors playing Iago in *Othello* have played evaluations and judgments: to *con*; to *surprise*; and the highly unplayable, to *lie*. Translate those evaluations into the active components separate from the information available.

Results

Avoid choosing actions that are the intended results of the actions you are playing. Take, for example, to *frustrate*. Frustration is the result of these actions: to *tease*, to *block*, to *tempt*, to *seduce*, or to *reject*. Some other results of actions: to *confuse*, to *sadden*, to *please*, to *impress*, to *provoke*, and to *motivate*. Save the results for your objective.

Does this eliminate the bulk of active verbs? Hardly. Human beings are capable of kazillions of actions, and nearly each one has a word for it. When there isn't, you can make one up. I liked "sarcasticize," and another one of my favorites is "to ironicize." Another is "to guilt-trip." Robert Lewis, Master acting teacher and original Group Theatre member, coined the word to "kitzle," meaning a kind of teasing/tickle. The fact that it sounds Yiddish makes its meaning more special to him.

Yiddish is a remarkable language for its emotions expressed through action. The word *kvell* means "to beam with pride." To *shmooze* means "to talk heart to heart." (It has been redefined by theatre-folk as meaning "to *pretend* to have a heart-to-heart while really trying to make social/business connections.") The sounds of the language evoke the spirit of the action. To *nosh* means "to nibble a snack." Perhaps this is why so many actors know *at least* one Yiddish word; the language itself is active.

Be wary that you don't make up words as a way to avoid developing the skill of thinking in terms of actions. The English language is astoundingly complex, with the largest vocabulary in the history of the world. Search first, then fill in the blanks.

The following chart contains five weak verbs and some stronger alternatives. Certainly, many are only shades of the same color, but it is the varying shades that make an interesting painting into a spectacular one. The difference between "to tell off" and "to chew out" are subtle, but your specific choice will bring your script interpretation to life in a way that absolutely no one else *can*.

WEAK VERB	STRONGER ALTERNATIVE		

To Tell:

You "tell" your doorman	To Command	To Teach	To Direct
you'll be back by 11.	To Order	To Suggest	To Cue In
You "tell" the gas	To Dictate	To Confirm	To Level With
station attendant you	To Notify	To Deny	To Cough Up
want 5 bucks worth.	To Convince	To Instruct	To Sketch
This is too pedestrian	To Promise	To Rebel	To Certify
an action to use in the	To Preach	To Contradict	To Witness
vast majority of	To Declare	To Lecture	To Spit Out
scenes, only for the	To Correct	To Confess	To Compare
simplest, most casual	To Clarify	To Lay Before	
lines.	To Prove	To Break the News to	

To Ask:

You "ask" a toll attendant	To Investigate	To Coax	To Coerce
how to get to I-95.	To Search Out	To Cajole	To Cross-examine
You "ask" a	To Pry	To Urge	To Petition
stranger if they have	To Entice	To Decipher	To Needle
change for a dollar.	To Verify	To Interview	To Grill
Again, as dull as "to	To Hunt For	To Dare	To Test
tell," but in the inter-	To Probe	To Challenge	To Beg
rogative tense.	To Seek	To Negotiate	To Nag
	To Plead	To Summon	To "Third Degree"

To Give:

This is too general to	To Bribe	To Pleasure	To Welcome
be strong even if what	To Befriend	To Barter	To Worship
is being given is	To Share	To Tempt	To Solve
powerful. Better to	To Present	To Seduce	To Flatter
find the SPECIFIC	To Promise	To Placate	To Bestow
action that expresses	To Help Out	To Suggest	To Award
that kind of giving, as	To Appease	To Humor	To Support
the accompanying verbs	To Invite	To Retreat	To Fork Over
define.			

WEAK VERB	STRONGER ALTERNATIVE		

To Show:

Too vague and ordinary	To Clarify	To Expose	To Re-create
to be strong. "Show	To Unmask	To Introduce	To Lampoon
and Tell" is best left	To Confide	To Entrance	To Sulk
to children. "Showing"	To Reveal	To Patronize	To Warn
how you feel is passive,	To Protest	To Inspire	To Propose
leaving the action of	To Offer	To Blame	To Demonstrate
response to the observer.	To Mock	To Baby	To Contradict
Instead, as in "to	To Guide	To Bring to Life	
give," choose precisely	To Nurse	To Shine a Light On	
HOW you want "to show."	To Assert	To Paint a Picture	

To Make (Feel):

Inspiring feelings in	To Startle	To Banish	To Make Love To
others is a great deal	To Appease	To Soothe	To Guilt-trip
of what all arts are	To Flirt	To Seduce	To Lord Over
about. However, using	To Dismiss	To Tickle	To Caress
"to make" as the heart	To Demean	To Destroy	To Insult
of your action is weak.	To Ridicule	To Disgrace	To Bruise
As in "to show," choose	To Arouse	To Goad	To Frighten
the specific action	To Terrify	To Torture	To Entrance
that will ELICIT that	To Cherish	To Charm	To Tease
emotional change in	To Repel	To Celebrate	To Plotz
your partner.	To Shut 'Em Up		

6 Application

OBJECTIVES, OBSTACLE, ACTION, BEAT

The Miracle Worker, by William Gibson, is an excellently crafted play about Helen Keller and her teacher, Anne Sullivan. Keller was a great American who, after contracting an acute fever when less than a year old, lost her sight and hearing. In the drama, her father, a publisher and former military captain, demands order in his Alabaman home, but communicating with and disciplining the willful Helen is nearly impossible. As Helen gets older—six and a half—she gets increasingly wild and potentially dangerous to her infant sister. After a series of ineffective governesses, Helen's mother, Kate, hires Anne Sullivan, a twenty-year-old, formerly blind, Irish orphan from the North. Anne and Captain Keller clash often as their views of "a woman's place" are irresolvably conflicted. Nevertheless, Anne's stubborn determination is precisely what Helen needs. Just previous to the scene we will study, Anne has shooed the family from the dining room, where Helen fiercely resisted Anne's attempt to get her to eat from her own plate with a spoon, rather than from everyone else's plate with her hands as she was accustomed. In more than five pages of stage directions, Gibson outlines the battle between Anne and Helen, who has been locked in the room by and with Anne. Meanwhile, Captain Keller, repelled both by the apparently violent relationship between the two as well as by Anne's independent demeanor, has decided to fire her. Only at the last minute, with Kate's continued pleas, does he relent.

Time: The 1860s
Place: A garden house near the Keller homestead.

CAPTAIN: I have decided to give you another chance.
ANNE: To do what?
CAPTAIN: To—remain in our employ. But on two conditions. I am not accustomed to rudeness in servants or women, and that is the first. If you are to stay, there must be a radical change in manner.
ANNE: Whose?
CAPTAIN: YOURS, young lady, isn't it obvious? And the second is that you persuade me there's the slightest hope of your teaching a child who flees from you now like the plague, to anyone else she can find in this house.
ANNE: There isn't.
KATE: What, Miss Annie?
ANNE: It's hopeless here. I can't teach a child who runs away.
CAPTAIN: Then—do I understand you—propose—
ANNE: Well, if we all agree it's hopeless, the next question is what—
KATE: Miss Annie. I am not agreed. I think perhaps you—underestimate Helen.
ANNE: I think everybody else here does.
KATE: She learns, she learns, do you know she began talking when she was six months old? She could say "water." Not really—"wahwah." "Wahwah," but she meant water, she knew what it meant, and only six months old, I never saw a child so bright, or outgoing—It's still in her, somewhere, isn't it? You should have seen her before her illness, such a good tempered child—
ANNE: She's changed.
KATE: Miss Annie, put up with it. And with us.
CAPTAIN: Us!
KATE: Please? Like the lost lamb in the parable, I love her all the more.
ANNE: Mrs. Keller, I don't think Helen's worst handicap is deafness or blindness. I think it's your love. And pity.
CAPTAIN: Now what does that mean?
ANNE: All of you here are so sorry for her you've kept her—like a pet, why, even a dog you housebreak. No wonder she won't

let me come near her. It's useless for me to try to teach her
language or anything else here. I might as well—
KATE: Miss Annie, before you came we spoke of putting her in an
asylum.

(ANNE turns back to regard her. A pause.)

ANNE: What kind of asylum?
CAPTAIN: For mental defectives.
KATE: I visited there. I can't tell you what I saw, people like—
animals, with—rats, in the halls, and— (She shakes her head
on her vision.) What else are we to do if you give up?
ANNE: Give up?
KATE: You said it was hopeless.
ANNE: HERE. Give up, why, I only today saw what has to be
done, to begin.

(She glances from KATE to CAPTAIN who stare, waiting.)

I—want complete charge of her.
CAPTAIN: You already have that. It has resulted in—
ANNE: No, I mean day and night. She has to be dependent on me.
KATE: For what?
ANNE: Everything. The food she eats, the clothes she wears, fresh
air, yes the air she breathes, whatever her body needs is a—
primer, to teach her out of. It's the only way, the one who lets
her have it should be her teacher. Not anyone who loves her,
you have so many feelings they fall over each other like feet,
you won't use your chances and you won't let me.
KATE: But if she runs from you—to us—
ANNE: Yes, that's the point. I'll have to live with her somewhere
else.
CAPTAIN: What!
ANNE: Till she learns to depend on and listen to me.
KATE: For how long?
ANNE: As long as it takes. I packed half my things already.
CAPTAIN: Miss—Sullivan!
ANNE: Captain Keller, it meets both your conditions. It's the one
way I can get back in touch with Helen, and I don't see how I
can be rude to you again if you're not around to interfere with
me.
CAPTAIN: And what is your intention if I say no!? Pack the other
half, for home, and abandon your charge to—to—

ANNE: The asylum?

I grew up in such an asylum. The state almshouse.
Rats—why, my brother Jimmie and I used to play with the rats
because we didn't have toys. Maybe you'd like to know what
Helen will find there, not on visiting days? One ward was full
of the—old women, crippled, blind, most of them dying, but
even if what they had was catching, there was nowhere else to
move them, and that's where they put us. There were younger
ones across the hall, prostitutes mostly, with T.B., and epileptic
fits, and a couple of the kind who—keep after other girls,
especially the young ones, and some insane. Some just had the
D.T.'s. The youngest were in another ward to have babies they
didn't want, they started at thirteen, fourteen. They'd leave
afterwards, but the babies stayed and we played with them,
too, though a lot of them had—sores all over from diseases
you're not supposed to talk about, but not many of them
lived. The first year we had eighty, seventy died. The room
Jimmie and I played in was the deadhouse, where they kept
the bodies till they could dig—

KATE (Closes her eyes): Oh my dear—!

ANNE: —the graves. No, it made me strong. But I don't think you
need send Helen there. She's strong enough. No, I have no
conditions, Captain Keller.

KATE: Miss Annie.

ANNE: Yes.

KATE: Where would you—take Helen?

In breaking down the scene, be wary not to choose an objective
without conflict. Although all the characters want to help Helen become part of the world, this interpretation eliminates conflict. *How*
they want to help Helen is conflicting. And how they overcome the
more immediate obstacles leading to this goal creates the conflict of
the scene. Also be equally aware that the obstacle you choose is *part*
of the scene. "I want Helen to learn" cannot be played because Helen is not in the scene.

Breaking the Scene into Objectives and Obstacles

Captain Keller

Objective: Examine his actions: He *concedes* (to let Anne remain in
their employ), he *lays down the law*, he *threatens*, he *commands*, he

challenges, and so on. His actions are directed at Anne. Some strong choices:

> Keller wants Anne to obey him.
>
> Keller wants her to confess her behavioral errors.
>
> Keller wants Anne to bow to his authority.

And there are many others limited only by the imagination and personal involvement of the actor playing him.

Obstacle: Look at what he has observed in Anne. If you were in his place, what might you assume she wanted? *The ideal obstacle is how you perceive your partner's objective.*

> Anne wants him to surrender his home.
>
> Anne wants to challenge his parenting abilities.
>
> Anne wants him to bow to her authority.

Kate Keller

Objective: First, note that Kate does not say a word for the first part of the scene. *The only reason we ever talk is because we want something we cannot immediately have.* She has succeeded in convincing her husband not to fire Anne. At this point she has no reason to talk. This does not mean she is without objective. Perhaps she wants to ensure that Anne and her husband do not get into another argument, and the obstacle is that they want to reenact the Civil War. But, for Kate, her first *playable* objective begins partway through the scene when Anne says, "There isn't."

Kate begins to *convince* Anne, *appeal* to her sympathies, *glorify* Helen's natural gifts, *plead* with her; Kate believes Anne can help Helen.

> Kate wants Anne to grant Helen one more chance.
>
> Kate wants to inspire Anne to the potential rewards.
>
> Kate wants Anne to promise to stay.

Obstacle: But what is the obstacle? Anne is not going anywhere. She is a twenty-year-old orphan with no home, no previous experience, impaired eyesight, and more than a thousand miles between her and anyone she has ever known. So if it is obvious that Anne is not leaving, then why is Kate trying so hard to get her to stay?

Remember, the obstacle is how your character *perceives* your partner's objective. *Kate has not read the play.* Anne, a survivor, knows how to play her audience and has convinced the Kellers that she is about to quit. Kate's obstacle:

Anne wants the Kellers to accept her resignation.

Anne wants the Kellers to concede it is hopeless.

Anne wants to convince the Kellers they are wasting their time.

Anne Sullivan

Objective: The most obvious objective is that Anne wants to open the world to Helen. But this is a trap. Helen is not part of this scene, and Anne's actions are not directed toward her. Although Helen is nearby, the scene is between Anne and the Kellers, so the objective must be focused on them.

There is another obvious choice, and it comes straight from the dialogue. In naturalistic American melodramas of the forties and fifties, it is common for the characters to come right out and state their objectives. Anne says, "I want complete charge of her." This only needs a little adjustment to make a playable objective because it must involve the partner(s).

Anne wants the Kellers to surrender complete charge of Helen.

Anne wants the Kellers to relinquish all control.

Anne wants to inspire the Kellers with hope.

Obstacle: Be careful never to choose an obstacle your character believes to be insurmountable. Even if *you* know it is impossible, it must seem believably possible to the character or else you make them fools for even trying.

A danger would be to choose what Anne points out to be an obstacle: "I don't think Helen's worst handicap is deafness or blindness. I think it's your love. And pity." This is a weak choice because there is nothing Anne can do to change the Kellers' love or pity. In fact, Anne is *using* those feelings to her advantage. The obstacle is grounded in the fact that the Kellers are Helen's parents. Taken one step further, what do the parents WANT?

> The Kellers want Anne to "train" Helen at home.
>
> The Kellers believe Helen is safest with them.
>
> The Kellers want to protect themselves from the pain of being separated from their child.

But wait. What does Anne's graphic description of the state almshouse in which she was raised have to do with getting control of Helen? When you read it, it makes truthful sense, but the actor playing Anne must be much more specific. Anne is basically saying, "I'd like you to surrender complete control of your daughter to me, and by the way, I used to play with dead babies for fun." Does this inspire confidence? The answer is in the obstacles.

Often, when we struggle to accomplish an objective in life, we battle what we *believe* to be the obstacle—only to discover later what the real obstacle is. From the beginning of this scene, Anne anticipates and perceives that her greatest obstacle is the Kellers' natural desire to parent their child and for Anne only to assist them with raising Helen. Only after attempting one tactic after another to battle this perceived obstacle does Anne recognize the *true* one. Anne *should* be able to call all the shots since she is the expert as well as their last hope after so many failures. Yet they remain stubborn. Only when she realizes that their obstinacy is supported by a belief that there is one last alternative, no matter how unpleasant, does Anne recognize the real obstacle. It becomes more important for Anne to combat this alternative than to overcome their desire for Helen to be near.

Although her objective remains the same, her tactics change because she finally recognizes the biggest obstacle. Now she must horrify and shame them enough to destroy that "unpleasant" option from their minds. The script supports this, because as soon as Kate says, "Oh my dear," Anne stops. Certainly, Anne can draw even more horrifying details, but when she succeeds in getting the tangible result of her goal—the Kellers' demonstrable horror—she needs no more. She then has one more action: to deflect their pity in order to refocus their attentions on Helen. The scene ends when Kate asks, "Where would you—take Helen?"

Breaking Down the Scene into Beats

After the objectives are chosen and the obstacles are identified, the scene can be broken down into crisp, specific actions that define the beats. For the purpose of this exercise:

> Captain Keller wants Anne to bow to his authority.
>
> Kate Keller wants Anne to grant Helen one more chance.
>
> Anne Sullivan wants the Kellers to surrender complete charge of Helen.

The beats of the scene are identified by a "//" in the text. When the actions change, a new beat begins. Happily, you will not agree with all or even most of the actions I've chosen, or even with the specific choices for beat changes. You will have your own interpretations based on your own unique insight into people, the world, and life experience; this is what keeps art fresh and in constant evolution. But note the *process* and that the actions outlined here are all strong and playable.

To Award	CAPTAIN: I have decided to give you another chance.
To Verify	ANNE: To do what?
	CAPTAIN: To—remain in our employ. But on two
To Lay Down	conditions. //I am not accustomed to
the Law	rudeness in servants or women, and that is
	the first. If you are to stay, there must be
	a radical change in manner.
	ANNE: Whose?//
To Dominate	CAPTAIN: YOURS, young lady, isn't it obvious?
	And the second is that you persuade me
	there's the slightest hope of your teaching a
	child who flees from you now like the plague,
	to anyone else she can find in this house.//
To Quit	ANNE: There isn't. [Note: It is tempting to choose "to bluff" because that is precisely what Anne is doing. However, that is a judgment of her actions, not the action itself. In order for her to bluff effectively, she must play the action "to quit" as fully as possible.]
To Probe	KATE: What, Miss Annie?

| | ANNE: It's hopeless here. I can't teach a child who runs away. |

To Examine CAPTAIN: Then—do I understand you—propose—
ANNE: Well, if we all agree it's hopeless, the next question is what—//

To Confront KATE: Miss Annie. I am not agreed. I think perhaps you—underestimate Helen.

To Chide ANNE: I think everybody else here does.//

To Inspire KATE: She learns, she learns, do you know she began talking when she was six months old? She could say "water." Not really—"wahwah." "Wahwah," but she meant water, she knew what it meant, and only six months old, I never saw a child so bright, or outgoing— It's still in her, somewhere, isn't it? You should have seen her before her illness, such a good tempered child—
ANNE: She's changed. //

To Beg KATE: Miss Annie, put up with it. And with us.

To Protest CAPTAIN: Us!
KATE: Please? Like the lost lamb in the parable, I love her all the more.//

To Condemn ANNE: Mrs. Keller, I don't think Helen's worst handicap is deafness or blindness. I think it's your love. And pity.
CAPTAIN: Now what does that mean?
ANNE: All of you here are so sorry for her you've kept her—like a pet, why, even a dog

To Abandon you housebreak.// No wonder she won't let me come near her. It's useless for me to try to teach her language or anything else here. I might as well—//

To Confess KATE: Miss Annie, before you came we spoke of putting her in an asylum.
(ANNE turns back to regard her. A pause.)

To Investigate ANNE: What kind of asylum?
To Disclose CAPTAIN: For mental defectives.
KATE: I visited there. I can't tell you what I saw, people like—animals, with—rats, in the halls, and—
(She shakes her head on her vision)

To Plead // What else are we to do if you give up?
To Correct ANNE: //Give up?

To Clarify	KATE: You said it was hopeless.
To Declare	ANNE: HERE. // Give up, why, I only today saw what has to be done, to begin.

(She glances from KATE to CAPTAIN who stare, waiting.)//

To Assert	I—want complete charge of her.
To Chastise	CAPTAIN: You already have that. It has resulted in—
	ANNE: No, I mean day and night. She has to be dependent on me.
To Search Out	KATE: For what?//
To Inspire	ANNE: Everything. The food she eats, the clothes she wears, fresh—air, yes, the air she breathes, whatever her body needs is a—primer, to teach her out of. It's the only way, the one who lets her have it should be her teacher. Not anyone who loves her, you have so many feelings they fall over each other like feet, you won't use your chances and you won't let me.
	KATE: But if she runs from you—to us—
	ANNE: Yes, that's the point. I'll have to live with her somewhere else.
	CAPTAIN: What!
	ANNE: Till she learns to depend on and listen to me.
	KATE: For how long?
	ANNE: As long as it takes. I packed half my things already.//
To Beat Down	CAPTAIN: Miss—Sullivan!
To "Clarence Darrow"	ANNE: Captain Keller, it meets both your conditions. It's the one way I can get back in touch with Helen, and I don't see how I can be rude to you again if you're not around to interfere with me.//
To Dare	CAPTAIN: And what is your intention if I say no!? Pack the other half, for home, and abandon your charge to—to—
To Challenge	ANNE: The asylum? I grew up in such an asylum. The state almshouse. Rats—why, my brother Jimmie and I used to play with the rats because
To Intrigue	we didn't have toys. // Maybe you'd like to know what Helen will find there, not on visiting days?//
To Haunt	One ward was full of the—old women, crippled, blind, most of them dying, but even if what

	they had was catching, there was nowhere else to move them, and that's where they put us. There were younger ones across the hall, prostitutes mostly, with T.B., and epileptic
To Share a Secret	fits, and a couple of the kind who//—keep after other girls, especially the young ones,
To Trivialize	// and some insane. Some just had the D.T.'s. The youngest were in another ward to have
To Condemn	babies they didn't want,// they started at thirteen, fourteen. They'd leave afterwards, but the babies stayed and we played with them, too, though a lot of them had—sores all over from diseases you're not supposed to
To Itemize	talk about, but not many of them lived.// The
To Attack	first year we had eighty, seventy died.// The room Jimmie and I played in was the deadhouse, where they kept the bodies till they could dig—
To Beg (her to stop)	KATE: *(Closes her eyes.)* Oh my dear—!
To Spurn	ANNE: —the graves.// No, it made me strong.//
To Guilt-trip	But I don't think you need send Helen there. She's strong enough.//
To Serve (as in tennis)	No, I have no conditions, Captain Keller.//
To Surrender	KATE: Miss Annie. ANNE: Yes.
To Accept	KATE: Where would you—take Helen?

Look at how the rhythms of the beat changes help heighten the dramatic impact of the scene. Notice how the changes become clipped and closer together before major plot turns. Before Anne asserts, "I want complete charge of her," the rhythm builds up speed. Also, the actions of her monologue build with the severity of her descriptions. This rhythm is continued until Kate finally grants Anne's request.

◢ Who's There?

Originating Character from Script

Creating characters is one of the greatest joys of acting. Through character we are transformed into another life, a life that experiences a world others can only imagine. A life that has permission to behave in myriad ways we don't allow ourselves. In character, we can murder a king, queen, prince, and then ourselves, and afterward, go home to feed the dog. It allows us to indulge secret facets of our personality and to discover others that we didn't know existed.

Sometimes we are required to play people who do things that are distasteful or frightening. They may be types of people we despise, or are alien to our understanding, or are "too close to home" for comfort. Or maybe we would rather play a different kind of character altogether than what has been written. So we "improve" them into something easier or more preferable. This is when characters begin to serve our personal needs, instead of us serving the needs of the character. Like parents who raise their children to satisfy their own needs rather than the reverse, if we create characters to serve our own desires they will grow stunted.

Every life form has requirements that will give it a strong heartbeat. You will create those necessary requirements when you begin with the script. There are two parts to breaking down the script's information to develop an effective, communicative character.

Part I: Creating a Biography

How well do you need to know a character in order to bring it to life? As well as you know yourself?

The comedian Andrea Martin created Dr. Enid Kinsey, a certified sexual therapist with a cable-television show. However, every time the therapist tries to say the word "sex," her face contorts, her body tenses, and the word stutters out of her mouth in spasms. It's hysterical. Nevertheless, if you were to ask the doctor if she were at ease with the subject, her answer would be, "Of course I am; I'm a s-s-exual therapist." It is through these unconscious actions that the audience learns more about her than she knows of herself.

How many things do you know about some family members or friends that they themselves have not caught on to yet? You know these things through objective observation of their actions and reactions. In a final performance, you can leave little to unconscious whims; you must play chosen actions. Part of those choices are the revealing expressions of which the character him- or herself may not even be aware—but *you* are.

Therefore, you do not need to know the character as well as yourself; you must know that character BETTER.

Think of what you need to know about a character in order to become him or her. Some elements are more crucial to one character than to another. A family play requires familial background. A historical play requires knowledge of its era. A social play requires understanding of your character's culture or civilization.

Suppose I were commissioned to write a biography of you because you have won your fourth Academy Award. Before I can really know who you are, what categories of biographical elements would I need to know?

Age	Temperament	Economic Class
Sex	Education	Social Status
Occupation	Sexuality	Morality
Family History	Relationships	Quirks
Religious Beliefs	Achievements	Intelligence
Hopes and Dreams	Nationality	Skills
Hobbies	Physical Abnormalities	Priorities
Fears and Phobias	Personal Rhythm	*Self-Image*
Past Traumas	Marital Status	*Projected Image*
Loves	Needs	*Perceived Image*

and so on.

The list is endless. "Favorite breakfast" might be inconsequential to know about you, but it might be essential if you are a nutritionist.

But where do you get the information? First and foremost: from the script. In the carefully chosen words of a playwright and the countless actions within a script, a foundation for a *character's biography* can be formed. The detail of this foundation comes from five specific places in the script. For the sake of this example, we will use the title role of Henrik Ibsen's *Hedda Gabler*.

What the Playwright Says About the Character

> She is a woman of twenty-nine. Her face and figure show breeding and distinction. Her complexion is pale and opaque. Her eyes are steel-gray and express a cold, unruffled repose. Her hair is an agreeable medium-brown, but not especially abundant. She wears a tasteful, somewhat loose-fitting negligee.

Information:

Twenty-nine years old

Aristocratic background

Attractive skin (pale was preferable then)

Seemingly cold and austere

Ordinary brown hair

Possibly pregnant.

The information the playwright lists contains the bare essentials necessary for the actor to understand the character. Why does Ibsen describe Hedda's hair if there seems to be nothing particularly unusual about it? Later you learn that Hedda is envious of her old schoolmate Thea Elvstead's full, blonde hair. Envy is a catalyst for many of the character's actions.

Reliability: Mostly reliable. After all, the playwright envisioned the character first and constructed the play with that vision. But even the playwright may not know the character as well as the actor who brings life to it. For example, Shaw writes a lengthy postscript to *Pygmalion* about how Eliza Doolittle leaves Higgins and marries Freddie. Yet her closing speech to Higgins, after saying good-bye, might seem to you more of an assertion of her equal value than a final farewell. In Shaw's screenplay adaptation from which *My Fair Lady* is taken, Eliza returns to Higgins. Shaw protested that he was bullied into this change. One might wonder if perhaps he recognized that he may not have created what he originally intended. Or perhaps Eliza is simply hammering the last nail in Higgins' coffin to teach him a lesson this time. Regardless of interpretation, it is important to remember that playwrights are as subjective as anyone else and that theatre relies on the collaboration of *all* artists' input. There is only one "final say": the production performance.

What the Character Says About Himself or Herself

> HEDDA: I sometimes think there's only one thing in this world
>   I'm really fitted for.
> BRACK: What's that, if I may ask?
> HEDDA: Boring myself to death.

Information:

Hedda is so bored she could die from it.

She is open and honest about her despair.

She feels responsible for her boredom.

She is frustrated with her inability to correct it.

Reliability: Somewhat reliable. First, people lie. Second, the view people have of themselves is limited by their personal insight. Just because Andrea Martin's sexual therapist *says* she is comfortable with sex doesn't mean it's true.

Whenever characters say something about themselves, what they say is fuel for biography. Even a lie can reveal truth—but weigh it within the subjective impressions of the character.

What Other Characters Say About the Character

> MISS TESMAN: After all, she's General Gabler's daughter. She was used to being spoiled when her father was alive. Do you remember how we used to see her galloping by? How smart she looked in her riding clothes!

Information:

Hedda is a general's daughter.

She was (and maybe still is) spoiled.

Her father is dead.

She rode horses boldly.

She was venerated by many people for her beauty.

Reliability: Somewhat reliable. For the same reasons that what your character says about himself or herself is subjective or easy to lie about, so is what others say. In addition, other characters may only know what your character wants them to know or what they wish to believe about themselves.

Aside from studying your own scenes, examine every scene in which your character is even casually mentioned. The view others have of your character reveals intentional, or unintentional, images that your character projects—both of which are invaluable sources.

The Character's Actions

This short scene from the last act reveals an enormous amount of information if it is analyzed well:

> TESMAN: But how could you do anything so unheard of?
>   [Burning the only copy of Lovberg's manuscript] What put it into your head? What possessed you? Do answer me—
> HEDDA (*Suppressing a scarcely perceptible smile*): I did it for your sake, Jorgen.
> TESSMAN: For my sake!
> HEDDA: This morning when you told me that he had read it to you—

TESSMAN: Yes, yes—what then?

HEDDA: You admitted that you were jealous of his work.

TESSMAN: Of course, I didn't mean that literally.

HEDDA: All the same—I couldn't bear the thought of anyone putting you in the shade.

TESSMAN (*In an outburst of mingled doubt and joy*): Hedda? Is this true? But—But—I have never known you to show your love like that before. Think of that!

HEDDA: Then—perhaps I'd better tell you that—just now—at this time— (*Violently breaking off.*) No, no; ask Aunt Juliane. She'll tell you about it. [Aunt Juliane speculated openly about Hedda's possible pregnancy.]

TESSMAN: Oh, I almost think I understand, Hedda. (*Clasping his hands together*) Great Heavens! Do you really mean it, eh?

HEDDA: Don't shout so loud. The servants will hear—

TESSMAN (*Laughing with irrepressible joy*): The servants—? Why, how absurd you are, Hedda! It's only my dear old Berte! Why, I'll run out and tell her myself!

HEDDA (*Clenching her hands in despair*): Oh god, I shall die—I shall die of all this!

Information:

She relishes power.

She is capable of great destruction.

She manipulates people.

She agonizes over her pregnancy.

She values class distinction.

She fears being the subject of talk.

She feels trapped in her circumstances.

She has an open and vulnerable heart.

Reliability: The *most* reliable. The cliché "actions speak louder than words" is never more apropos than in character development. Characters may lie and playwrights may lose objectivity, but actions are the truth.

Interpreting character actions is the most important and subjective part of script analysis. What the character does and *does not* do reveals the most information, but it must be examined with a sharp eye. Too often, actors accept a character's action simply because it makes better theatre, or is necessary to further the plot, or just "because it's in the script." But the fine actor never settles for less than truth.

Hedda succeeds in complicating Tessman in her destructive plan. He accepts that he was the motivation for her actions and, as an unwitting accomplice, must support and defend Hedda. Why then does she (nearly) confess her pregnancy, something she feels she "shall die from" acknowledging? Because the script says so?

When she thrusts responsibility on Tessman, she believes and anticipates that he will react with great guilt and painful duty. Rather, he becomes overjoyed that she has finally demonstrated love for him. (In one translation, he rejoices that she has finally begun addressing him by his first name.) Expecting anger and pain from him, she instead is showered with his affection, even though she does not want it. This simple man gives her his heart and soul and is so easily pleased by the simplest gestures, yet she gives him nothing. Perhaps she is so affected by his simple joys that she elects to share the rest. Perhaps, being overwhelmed by his immense and unconditionally childlike love for her, she begins to feel a kind of affection for him. Perhaps her own conscience, as exhibited many times earlier in her confessions to Judge Brack and her respect of Lovberg's need to confess to her, forces her to pay penance for her wrong.

Hedda Gabler, a character amateurishly dismissed as witchlike and evil, has an open heart.

No matter *how* you interpret her action, it must be interpreted. Your interpretation may take weeks to crystallize, but you will be rewarded with a deeper insight and stronger vision of the character whose soul you must bring to life.

With careful study, these first four places in the script will reveal all the important information the playwright has chosen. Use this information for your character biography and you will have an accurate foundation fully supported by the script. However, "accuracy" is not the prime goal for an artist—creation is.

The Intangibles

Imagination

Instinct

Inspiration

Impulse

Identification

Intuition

Insight

One of the major thematic ideas throughout *Hedda Gabler* is that women had limited choices in 1890s society. Her most powerful options come only through her interaction, control, and manipulation of men. Also, there is the issue of Hedda's pregnancy, a fact she finds repulsive and denies vehemently. Given these details, how important is it to know what Hedda's relationship with her mother was? Since a mother is usually a young woman's first female role model, it is tremendously important. Yet you will not find one mention of Madame Gabler in any translation. Ibsen did not feel this was crucial for the audience to know, but the modern actor who understands human psychology and the importance of family history will hunger for this information to complete Hedda's portrait.

This is when your creativity takes full force. These are the "I" words because they come from you. Perhaps you can *imagine* the General's wife, properly walking six paces behind her husband, while Hedda, six paces behind her, is gripping the cold glove of her governess. Perhaps you can *identify* with Hedda's frustration with women's roles and her anger at her mother's inaction. Perhaps somewhere, somehow, you get an idea that Hedda's mother died when she was very young. The *inspiration* is that she was abandoned to the severe care of her distant father.

These are the intangibles that come from the depths of talent. This is creativity. *This is what makes the difference between an artisan and an artist, craft versus creation.*

Reliability: Total—*and dangerous.* The problem is that these intangibles come from a deep place that is as closely related to personal need as it is to artistic expression. If your *identification* with Hedda is very strong, you may choose that her marriage to the insufferably dull Jorgen Tessman is a happy one, because *your* marriage is. Your *intuition* may suggest that Hedda is frightened of the guns she consistently plays with because *you* are frightened of guns.

From the intangible places, your most inspired and profound choices will be made, and so will the most subjectively dangerous.

Then why use these subjective areas if the previous four places

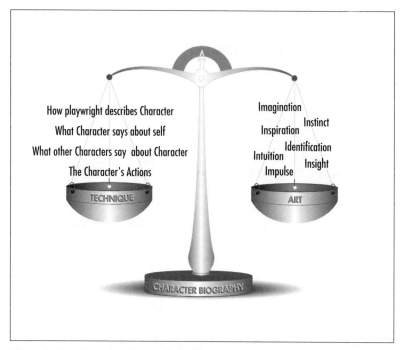

Figure 7–1   Character Biography Scale

to look in the script develops the most accurate representation of character? Because aside from being the most accurate, they are also the most mechanical. Wax museums can be astonishingly accurate, but do you believe that the figures are alive? If you've ever seen a body in an open casket, did it really look "asleep"?

The only way to create life is *with* life. Your soul, where your talent lives, is crucial to creating another breathing being on stage. The intangibles come from the soul.

To discern between artistic inspiration and personal subjectivity, balance the first four places against the fifth. Picture it like a scale (see Figure 7–1).

Check one side of the scale with the other. Your genuine artistic inspirations will have been triggered by the script. Even your identification and unique insight into the human condition have been sparked as relevant to this play by some minute detail you read. Go back to the script and comb for supporting details. They're probably there. If you can't find anything specific, you may still be making a strong choice so ask yourself: Do the actions of the character consistently support this instinctive conclusion without contradiction? If not, examine yourself. Do you have any personal reason you may want the character to have these qualities? You may still not have an answer. You may never have an answer. But at least your choices will be made intentionally and as objectively as any artist can, and your chances for profound biographical character development is strongest.

And it still doesn't make a character. . . .

Part II: Creating the Character

As far as the world is concerned, we are the sum total of our actions. We may have wonderful intentions, deep feelings, brilliant ideas, clever wit, and more love in our hearts than a litter of puppies, but unless we do something about it, it doesn't count. Even if we *talk* about all these things, without accompanying deeds, our talk is useless. During every political election, we hope that the "talk" will be supported by actions. When it isn't, no "talk" will outweigh that.

Characters can only be communicated by the observable actions you choose for them. No matter how strongly you believe, feel, understand, and identify with your character, no one will perceive it until you DO something. A script gives only the outline of actions; you animate it moment to moment. So take your biographical elements and translate them, as Stanislavsky told us to do, into playable character elements.

To make the final translation from biography to tangible character, you need only one word: *THEREFORE*. With the biographical information you have gleaned from the script, take it one step further. He or she is X; *therefore* he or she does Y. Every personality trait is expressed to the world through action. The caregiver *nurtures, soothes, caresses*. The troublemaker *complains, demands, interferes*. The joyful *celebrate, joke, beam*. With every biographical element you discover for your character, there are actions that outwardly express it. When you choose those, you are in the final stages of communicating character.

You will also find that by playing these actions, you are most easily transformed into character. There is a Psychology 101 lesson that explains that if you want someone to be your friend, get them to do you a favor. One might think that it is more useful to *offer* a favor, but tests have demonstrated the opposite. The reason is something called "cognitive dissidence." You cannot continually do one action while thinking something in conflict with it. If you *do* a favor for someone, you inevitably begin to believe, "Gee, I must like this guy if I'm doing him a favor." It follows that if you fidget in your seat, startle at the slightest noise, dart your eyes around the room, and giggle at everything anyone says, you'll begin to believe, "Gee, I must be a nervous wreck." And more important, the audience observing all these actions will note, "Gee, what a nervous wreck."

The "translation table" that follows uses some of the information gathered from the biography of Hedda Gabler and translates it into playable actions.

Biographical Elements		Character Elements
I am, have, was, feel, want (the intellectual)	*Therefore→*	*I do.* (the observable)
My father was a general.	*Therefore→*	I command, I march, I play with guns, I follow decorum, I stand erect, I confront, I order, I dominate, I strategize, I lord over, I dictate, I retaliate, I advise, I ride horses, I proclaim.
I am venerated for my beauty.	*Therefore→*	I flirt, I model, I prance, I posture, I dress well, I entertain, I welcome, I preen, I smile, I tease, I compete, I ride horses.
I seem cold and austere.	*Therefore→*	I avoid eye contact, I criticize, I maintain distance, I hide my emotions, I guard, I judge, I scold, I shun, I ignore, I patronize.
My heart is vulnerable.	*Therefore→*	I confess, I inspire, I cry out, I console, I apologize, I relent, I reveal, I empathize, I welcome, I entrust, I plead, I seek help, I dream, I laugh, I flirt, I bleed.

I am bored.	*Therefore→*	I taunt, I fantasize, I toy with people's lives, I seek adventure, I challenge, I pace, I play with guns, I fidget, I joke, I flirt, I tease, I entertain guests, I eavesdrop.
I am power hungry.	*Therefore→*	I command, I seduce, I dominate, I play with guns, I overtake others' lives, I defy, I escape, I demand, I plot, I command, I seek weak spots, I attack, I assert, I defend, I ensnare.
My mother died when I was young.	*Therefore→*	I walk heavily like my father, I deflect contact, I renounce my pregnancy, I distance myself, I protect my emotions, I fight for power, I vie for attention.

You may find many contradictions when you research characters, especially those from modern plays. This is because real people are filled with contradictions; only cartoon characters are consistently one-dimensional.

You may also find the same character element supporting more than one biographical element. This is not a repetition but an emphasis, a clue to your character's priorities. Some people eat simply to survive. "I am a mammal," *therefore* "I eat food." But for other people, eating fulfills many needs. "I am a mammal," *therefore* "I eat food" joins with "I adore physical sensation," *therefore* "I eat food"; "I am alone and lonely," *therefore* "I eat food"; "My mother always fed me to show her love," *therefore* "I eat food. . . ." For these people, eating becomes much more crucial to who they are. They do not "eat," they *relish, luxuriate, infuse, savor,* and *make love to* their food.

As you complete Hedda's character breakdown, you realize that her father's pistols are more than playthings that distract from her boredom; they are also symbols of her father, representations of absolute power, defense against predators, and guarantors of her destiny. Does she "give" one to Lovberg at the end of the third act, or does she *bestow*, *grant*, *surrender*, or *award* him with it? What does she do when she is told there is not enough money for a proper stable of horses?

Read over separately the two columns of the Biography/Character example. Each gives similar information, but the first column is what you only understand, and the second is what you see yourself *doing*. The second column consists of observable actions the audience can see; the first has conclusions that result from observation.

There is a fringe benefit to doing this. If you have difficulty translating all scenes and beats into strong, playable actions, this process creates a toolbox full of actions—*tailor-made to your character*.

Allow the audience to decipher who you are; it is one of the captivating joys of attending the theatre. As you play for them what you *do*, they will actively puzzle out the person you *are* and maintain involvement, identification, and fascination with a living, dynamic performance. And you will have succeeded in taking an abstract, loosely outlined, fictional being, and giving it breathing life, sympathetic depth, and human soul.

8 　 Doorways into the Audience

The audience must feel a connection to the play for it to make its strongest statement. That connection, or relevance, is determined by its universal truths, and those truths are recognized by its audience. Unless the play contacts the present life of those watching, it becomes merely a performed dialogue of distant ideas and abstract feelings. A friend of mine felt some of this distance from Euripides' *Medea* until she herself went through a violent divorce and found she was injuriously using her own children in order to torment her husband. Suddenly, the play had a powerful meaning for her because it reached her on personal levels. It is this kind of contact that dramatists strive for in order to make lasting, life-changing theatre.

The four elements that astrologists divide the twelve zodiac signs into—Fire, Earth, Air, and Water—suggest four doorways to an individual's personality. Fire signs are governed by their *spirit*; earth signs are governed by the *physical world*; air signs are governed by their *intellect*; and water signs are governed by their *emotions*. In an argument, it is very difficult when one person is speaking from the mind while the other person is speaking from the heart. The "fight scene" in Neil Simon's *Barefoot in the Park* shows exactly that. If Simon had included a third character who "speaks" from the body, it would have been a <u>bloody</u> *Barefoot in the Park*.

Playwrights use three doorways—heart, mind, and body—to communicate to the audience. Scripts can reach the mind through rational thought, the heart through emotional connection, or the body through audience involvement (which is different from "audience participation"). Most scripts are weighted toward mind, heart, or body, although virtually all good scripts contact all three. Bertoldt Brecht is often looked at as a purely intellectual playwright, but he could not have achieved such global appeal if he solely spoke to only one facet of life. His term "Verfremdungseffekt" has been translated as "alienation effect" and used as rationale that his plays only reach the mind.

Perhaps a more suitable translation would be "to-make-distant effect," but this is a clumsy phrase not catchy enough for academic jargon. Nevertheless, for actors, this is a more active explanation of what his plays try to do. He believed that when an audience was so emotionally involved that they were cathartically purged by the action, then ideas were only mental manipulations; their experience was passively complete; and energies that *should* be spent evaluating and then changing the social ills reflected in the play were used up. In order to tip the scales more toward the intellectual than the emotional, he distanced the audience enough through abstraction and a deemphasis on character psychology to make their connection more active and intellectual. By maintaining the most effective distance, we *recognize* the truth of the characters as a people rather than *identify* with one character moment to moment.

Depending on the script's intended statement, playwrights choose the strongest doorway(s) for reaching their audience at a particular point. Suppose you hired a lawyer to defend you against a false accusation. How confident would you be if the bulk of your lawyer's argument centered around what a lovable person you are, how much anguish this accusation is causing you, and ended with a poem about the glories of freedom? Is this the best doorway to the jurors' *minds*?

Suppose also that (insert fantasy lover here) were proposing to spend the rest of your lives together. Would this be best executed in a bound document indexed with: (1) what we share in common, (2) the financial benefits of partnership, and (3) a two-column worksheet on the Pros and Cons of our mutual commitment? And if you wanted to sexually arouse (insert same fantasy lover) one Saturday night, would you discuss the merits of physical expression or sing "People Will Say We're in Love"? Just as you choose the best method to make your point, so does the playwright. And the actor must choose the strongest techniques to communicate those specialized moments of a script.

Part I: Reaching the Mind

In the 1500s while Russia was still battling invading Mongols, Italy was evolving the Renaissance. When Constantinople fell, fleeing scholars and scientists arrived in Italy, bringing lost arts and information from ancient civilizations. Italy's productive economy and flourishing city-states—not to mention being the center of Christianity—became the model for the rest of Europe. When England, already adopting Renaissance sensibilities, defeated the Spanish Armada, it too became a center of focus. Their strengths were parliamentary government and religious philosophy. Protestantism, which had evolved with Henry VIII (so he could get a Catholic-forbidden divorce), spurred enormous debate on the meaning of God, divine law, and the nature of human freedom and social class.

It's no wonder England made the first wide use of a little German invention called the printing press. Their devotion to ideas required a strong language to communicate, and that language has become the most widely spoken in the history of the world. Because of its many verbal tributaries (German, Celtic, French, and others), it has a rich array of sounds, rhythms, and intonations. The enormous variety of socioeconomic classes and national origins of its speakers builds the English vocabulary to the largest of all languages: It is estimated to have approximately two million words. How many words can you think of that mean "happy"? You won't match it in any other language. The English pride themselves on their language because as a tool it can convey a wealth of thought clearly without resorting to physical expressions or abstract imagery.

Language is a tool of the mind. The richer the language, the less need to communicate with screaming, destruction, tears, or physical demonstration. The reason "the pen is mightier than the sword" is because a powerfully organized speech can cut deeper or inspire greater accomplishment than our animalistic physicality can. If you want to reach someone's mind, you won't find a better way than language, nor a richer language than English.

Legal systems use language because the law is philosophical. Emotional reactions interfere with the logic of philosophy. A great lawyer may become impassioned, but it is through the passion of an idea, not the indulgence of his or her own heart. And this is how the actor brings power and drama to plays that reach the mind. For actors to bring mind-reaching scripts to dramatic life, they must fully understand, appreciate, and most important, excite themselves about the great *ideas* of the play.

Inherit the Wind by Lawrence and Lee, *Whose Life Is It, Anyway?* by Clark, and *Arcadia* by Stoppard are examples of plays that reach the mind. Most courtroom dramas attempt to reach the mind. Social and political subjects often use this doorway. Any character who is attempting to convince you or an audience of a concept, great idea, or injustice most likely will do so through reaching your mind. Certainly, they may shout, cry, or celebrate, but the energy of that emotion is through the elevating power of a huge belief. In these plays or speeches, the *idea* is too large to be merely a personal problem; it is a great, universal truth that the character has become part of—not the other way around.

A danger, of course, is playing this style in a purely intellectual, detached manner. We have enough emotionless, synthesized voices in our answering machines, supermarkets, and the lovely "woman" who tells us our seatbelts are unfastened. Joan of Arc was not a computer chip. Yet it is equally dangerous to, in an effort to humanize her, play her emotional and self-indulgent. Saint Joan did not cry for herself; she was lifted to cry for her country, for God, and for justice. The passion of her conviction fuels her emotions; her emotional state does not bubble up into a conviction. The former creates an unparalleled leader of people; the latter makes a hysterical teenage girl.

The English (inventors of English) evolved a culture through this highly communicative language. The concise, expressive, and antibarbaric use of well-organized speech and writing fueled one of the most powerful and culturally enriching civilizations since the Greeks.

Of all playwrights who primarily reach the mind, Bernard Shaw is probably the most verbal—he was certainly the most prolific—and a perfect example for our study. Although his plays are often very funny and sometimes moving, he uses his gift for words and idea organization to open the door to the audience's mind. You would hardly call his plays "wacky" or "tearjerkers"; he did write astonishingly articulate and fascinating arguments about social class and gender conflicts that created a great deal of controversy and combative response from his audiences.

Yet, too often, I hear students tell me that they love to read Shaw but can't stand to see it on stage. This is usually because their only exposures to Shaw in performance were acted or directed by others who also thought his plays were such rich reading that actors need only "read well" to perform them. The performers posture across the stage overarticulating in an effort to sound intelligent, playing very few actions—mostly to *preach, lecture, teach, explain, opine,* and *discuss.* How could Shaw's plays have stimulated such passionate controversy if they only presented dry discussion?

Shaw loved good theatre and used its active power to dramatize ideas, as well as to tell a good story. His characters' objectives are less about personal feelings and more about impassioned beliefs. (Even his characters' romantic encounters have a profound "logic" to them.) The actions they use to change the world or another's doctrine are as varied and exciting as any other strong character. But Shaw becomes artificial, irrational, and talky when actors mistakenly try to find the emotion in their character's objectives *first* before discovering the passions inspired by their character's *convictions.* It is those heartfelt convictions that ignite a personal objective.

Below is a "speech" from the third act of *Man and Superman,* which Shaw labels "a comedy and a philosophy." This act has often been performed as an independent play entitled *Don Juan in Hell* because, well, that's what it's about. This excerpt is a dream sequence *Man and Superman*'s main character, Jack Tanner, has while trying to escape "the life force." ("The life force" is a theory prevalent in most of Shaw's plays—see Chapter 11.) The characters are:

> Ana: the embodiment of the life force who looks remarkably like Ann, the woman from whom Jack is struggling to escape
>
> A Statue: come to life, which looks remarkably like someone who helped get Jack into this mess
>
> Don Juan: a remarkable Jack lookalike, and
>
> The Devil: who looks like the devil

Don Juan and Ana, both lives ended and in Hell, confront each other about gender relations. There is an eternal conflict in the life force between men and women. Don Juan, the archetypal free man, has defended the fleeing reaction men have when women change from being embodiments of all that is beautiful to "unscrupulous beasts of prey" hunting husbands. But Ana, wise from a long life, doesn't let him get away with it.

> DON JUAN: I ran away from it. I ran away from it often. In fact I became famous for running away from it.
> ANA: Infamous, you mean.
> DON JUAN: I did not run away from you. Do you blame me for running away from the others?
> ANA: Nonsense, man. You are talking to a woman of 77 now. If you had had the chance, you would have run away from me too—if I had let you. You would not have found it so easy with me as with the others. If men will not be faithful to their homes and their duties, they must be made to be. I daresay you all want to marry lovely incarnations of music and painting and poetry. Well, you can't have them, because they don't exist. If flesh and blood is not good enough for you, you must go without. That's all. Women have to put up with flesh-and-blood husbands—and little enough of that too sometimes: and you will have to put up with flesh-and-blood wives. (The DEVIL looks dubious. The STATUE makes a wry face.) I see you don't like that, any of you, but it's true, for all that; so if you don't like it you can lump it.

At first reading, you may only appreciate its clarity and message. It may sound like a "speech." In many ways it is (it's called *rhetoric* if you need a more proper term), but it is also the fight of one character trying to change another.

First, of course, it is most important to understand what she is trying to say. This isn't Jacobean English, so the sentences are pretty clear—but *what* is she saying? Don Juan's argument is that men flee because they are in search of their ideal woman, and when men discover that a woman is not their ideal, naturally they run away. Ana refutes the preposterousness of seeking any form of "perfection" and asserts that no human being, man or woman, epitomizes anyone's ideal. His lengthy protestations, according to Ana, only rationalize an elongated adolescence.

You might summarize the idea and tone of Ana's speech: "Grow up and cut the bull****!" *If you can paraphrase the overall idea(s) of a speech, you're halfway there.*

Next, what is the best objective for you as Ana? One option is suggested simply by the summary paraphrased above: I want you to abandon your childishness. Or I want you to take responsibility, or wake up to reality, or face the truth once and for all, or many, many others.

The obstacle? He wants you to sympathize with men's dilemma, or recognize the impossibility of sexual relations, or face HIS truth once and for all.

Before the innumerable choices for actions can be made, you need to find a connection with Ana's passion. Can you relate to it? It only takes compassion. How many people today justify promiscuity (and lament their shallow existence) by the search for the "perfect" match? How many people suffer eating disorders, surgical alteration, and chemical ingestion in order to mold themselves into the contemporary concept of "perfection" just to meet a partner? Does it infuriate you when your lover refuses to take any mature responsibility for his or her side of the relationship? At some point, the anger at what has happened to you advances to a larger anger at media propaganda, gender bias, or social prejudice. You speak not only for yourself but for your buddy who spends thousands of dollars he doesn't have on hair implants, your girlfriend who was hospitalized with anorexia, your child who stays home alone because of self-esteem undermined by bigotry.

This anger transcends into a greater rage at a universal wrong. It is these electric, all-encompassing emotions that fueled the powerful oratories of Dr. Martin Luther King, Abraham Lincoln, Winston Churchill, Mahatma Gandhi, and every great leader. When emotions are not self-indulgent, they infect others and incite listeners to action. This is why the mind is a *door*; that door doesn't *only* reach your intelligence but becomes the entrance to the rest of you.

Once the choices of objective and obstacle, and the personal connection to the character's stakes are found, the action/beats can then be explored. The beats in scripts that reach the mind are determined by the idea. When the idea changes, the beat changes. The action for the beat is chosen as the strongest one that this particular character makes to convey that idea.

In the lines preceding Ana's speech, Don Juan attempts to *flatter* her: He claims that she must be exceptional, because he did not run from her.

DON JUAN: I did not run away from you. Do you blame me for
running away from the others?

The first *idea* in Ana's speech is that frivolous attempts may work on
blushing girls, but not on a woman.

ANA: Nonsense, man. You are talking to a women of 77 now. If
you had had the chance, you would have run away from me,
too . . .

An action to express the idea strongly: to *ridicule*. (Reminder: these
are potential choices, not "definitive" actions.)
The next idea comes before the end of the sentence—Ana re-
minds him that she is a formidable foe.

. . . if I had let you. You would not have found it so easy with me
as with the others.

Action: to *strut*.
Then she takes over the argument. First she outlines the reality
of marriage and the shortcomings of husbands:

If men will not be faithful to their homes and their duties, they
must be made to be. I daresay you all want to marry lovely
incarnations of music and painting and poetry.

Action: to *unmask*.
Next idea: She zeros in on his illusion:

Well, you can't have them, because they don't exist.

Action: to *shake up*.
Next idea: She spells out the reality of human limitations versus
romantic ideals.

If flesh and blood is not good enough for you, you must go
without. That's all. Women have to put up with flesh-and-
blood husbands—

Action: to *pronounce sentence*.
Now, Shaw and writers who reach the mind often have a *parenthetical action*, which temporarily interrupts the build of a surrounding

action. For example, if you're advising your sister while your son is fiddling with her bric-a-brac, your dialogue might be:

> And if you stand up to the board of directors and make your—
> Tommy, put that down before you break it!—make your position
> clear, then they have no choice but to acknowledge the problem.

Your action for the line is to *advise*, but interrupting it temporarily is the action to *scold*. When you return to advising, you pick up right where you left off. Intelligent dialogue often has these "side-note comments" in the midst of a continuous idea/beat. They are wonderful places for humor, opinion, sarcasm, or any other less-than-intellectual action that reveals the most human sides of characters.

We broke off in Ana's speech just before a parenthetical action surrounded by her Pronouncing Sentence:

> —and little enough of that too sometimes.

Action: to *demean*.

And then she returns to Pronouncing Sentence without so much as a hesitation:

> and you will have to put up with flesh-and-blood wives.

This is how parenthetical actions work. They are "parenthetical" be-cause they are dropped in the middle of an ongoing idea (making sense yet?) without interrupting its momentum. Since they are in-dependent ideas, they suggest independent actions.

The Devil and Statue react, which instigates the idea that she knows this truth is unpleasant to them, but she will not rescind.

> I see you don't like that, any of you, but it's true, for all that; so if
>   you don't like it

Action: to *challenge*.

> you can lump it.

Action: to *brush off*.

In this one, short (for Shaw) speech, we have a woman, wise from a long life, who is infuriated by the irresponsible childishness of men. In confronting a former and infamous lover, she ridicules, struts, unmasks, shakes up, pronounces sentence (demeans), challenges, and brushes off. If the actor playing her has connected to the passion, then her performance cannot be dry or dull. She will fill the moment with intriguing, emotionally charged actions that do not sacrifice the articulate clarity of the script's ideas.

Can you imagine the disservice if the actor chose to find the emotional connection first in an intellectual exchange? Suppose she connected first with the rejection, or abandonment. Her actions might be: to shut up, to belittle, to complain, to plead, to insult, and to attack—IF she found that much variety. Oh yes, the idea would be thrown in somewhere along the way. But the actor who allows the idea to *lead* her choices will choose strong, varied actions that use language and ideas as well as a sculptor uses hammer and chisel.

Note: Nowhere is your voice and speech work more important than when you play scripts that reach the mind. This is true not only because the words must be heard, but also because the vocal instrument must *play* these words like a great musician plays notes. Words are abstract images for great (and not-so-great) concepts. The word *compassion* is meaningless to a Korean, and their word for it becomes meaningless to the Portuguese. But the *idea* the vocal sound conjures to those who recognize it is enormous.

What happens to the word *Maria* when Tony attaches a human being to it in *West Side Story*? "*Say it loud and there's music playing; say it soft and it's almost like praying.*" How the actor strums the word can communicate more than anything read. Play with the hard *B*, *T*, and *D* in the word *bastard*. (Out loud, no one is listening.) Or think of Sleeping Beauty when you say the word *princess*. Now try saying *abscess* the same way. Better yet, go through your favorite list of swearwords and find how many sounds suit your emotional state when you say them.

Shakespeare used the malleability of English to convey a huge variety of emotional states. From *A Midsummer Night's Dream*:

LYSANDER: Where art thou proud Demetrius? Speak thou now.
DEMETRIUS: Thou runaway, thou coward, art thou fled?
Speak! In some bush? Where dost thou hide thy head?

Listen to the hard *D*s, *T*s, and *K*s. Use them. Let the *D* in *proud* be independent from the *D* in *Demetrius*.

> DEMETRIUS: O Helen, goddess, nymph, perfect, divine! . . . O
> let me kiss
> This princess of pure white, this seal of bliss!

Listen to the whispery *S*s, and soft *WH*.

> HELENA: O weary night! O long and tedious night
> Abate thy hours: shine, comforts, from the East . . .
> And sleep, that sometimes shuts up sorrow's eye,
> Steal me a while from mine own company.

Use the long vowels, the *E*s, *I*s, and *O*s to communicate her exhaustion. Try saying it with the same anger as Lysander's speech above; doesn't really work, does it? Playing Shakespeare is the perfect practice for learning how to use language as a tool.

When you analyze scripts that reach the mind, the overall ideas are paramount; the ideas are expressed through the actions; the words are symbols for those ideas; and the sounds are the flesh and bones of the words.

Part II: Reaching the Heart

The most universal human experience is emotion. We all share the desire to be happy. Anger fuels hostile aggression or productive assertion. Jealousy festers like cancer. Without love, we slowly deteriorate until we die. The expression of those emotions—laughter, tears, knit brows, trembling hands—are as universally communicative in the Kalahari as they are in K-Mart.

Emotions are also the most elusive, amorphous, and intangible of human experiences. Even Stanislavsky abandoned trying to reach the actor's emotions directly; his more evolved teachings concluded that emotions must be coaxed through imagination and physicalization. Playwrights who strive to reach the heart must use similar "ploys." Writing dialogue such as "This is so sad" or "I'm as happy as can be" or even "I love you" may convey the idea of sadness or happiness or love but will not arouse the genuine emotions of an audience.

Emotions in an audience are reached through their compassion. In order for compassion to be aroused, there must be something familiar. When things are peculiar or alien, we may laugh or fear or become intrigued, but we do not feel compassion because we have no point of reference.

The challenge for playwrights who reach the heart is to get an audience to feel for the same things the writer does. As Hermia in *A Midsummer Night's Dream* says about her father's disapproval of Lysander, "I would my father look'd but with *my* eyes"; playwrights who choose this doorway want you to "feel but with *their* hearts." It is nearly impossible through the analytical, intelligent discussion that is used in plays that reach the mind. Although emotional response is uniquely personal, playwrights capitalize on a variety of universal human experiences that evoke emotion.

Atmosphere

Atmosphere is one of the most direct ways to reach the heart. Many plays from the middle of this century were referred to as "kitchen-sink dramas" because the atmosphere was that of common domestic life. The setting of a play is crucial to acting choices. If you are arguing with your mate, how does that action adjust if you enter a great cathedral? Or a penthouse cocktail party? Or a moonless spring night when the sky is blanketed with stars? Do you have any recordings of ocean waves or crickets or rainstorms that you like to play when napping or reading or making love? For a romantic dinner, is a Sousa march the most appropriate accompaniment to your candles?

To ignore the atmosphere of a play is to ignore the single greatest advantage of live versus filmed performance: The audience is there with you. Master teacher and actor Michael Chekhov wrote in *To the Actor*, "The atmosphere [of a play] inspires the actor and unites the audience with him."

Unfortunately, it has become popular to dismiss the atmosphere within a script as useless and unplayable ("just spell 'mood' backwards"). Certainly, production designers are the most invaluable in bringing the script's atmosphere to its most tangible life, but this does not mean that the actor has no use for it. You cannot finalize your choices in the fluorescent-lit rehearsal space and expect them to unite with the designer's work if they were made independent of it. Skillfully interpreted, the atmosphere of a script can reveal the soul that reaches your and the audience's heart.

Few plays that speak to the heart do so without specific atmospheres. Your acting technique most likely makes use of "given circumstances" or some concept addressing the where of the play. This is because we behave and respond differently depending on these circumstances. The specific locations and periods are the factual ingredients; the atmospheres are the interpretive flavors.

For example, Arthur Miller subtitled *Death of a Salesman* as *Certain Private Conversations in Two Acts and a Requiem*. The atmosphere suggests the intimate nature of the play in spite of its tragic size. He begins the play with music—a proven method for creating mood: *"Act One: a melody is heard, played upon a flute. It is small and fine, telling of grass and trees and the horizon."* Miller lulls us into a pastoral feeling. Then the curtain rises:

> *Before us is the Salesman's house. We are aware of towering, angular shapes behind it, surrounding it on all sides. Only the blue light of the sky falls upon the house and forestage; the area shows an angry glow of orange. As more light appears, we see a solid vault of apartment houses around the small, fragile-seeming home. An air of the dream clings to the place, a dream rising out of reality. . . . The entire setting is wholly, or, in some places, partially transparent.*

Here the talent of designers becomes indispensable. But theatre is collaborative; your choices are made in concert with all of the artists involved.

The first action after the set description is *"Willy Loman, the Salesman, enters and as he crosses the stage to the doorway of the house, his exhaustion is apparent."* Soon, he puts down his heavy sample bags.

There are many ways to enter exhausted and overburdened, but the actor who is oblivious to the atmosphere established beforehand will create only a fraction of this powerful image. Like the house, Willy is becoming entombed by progress. He struggles to keep his own dream when the surrounding world infects him. Is he merely exhausted or is he being eaten alive? Are the bags heavy or do they contain the greater weight of crippled hopes that no longer carry themselves? If you acknowledge the apartment houses burying your home and hope, you will create the exhaustion and burden far more effectively than if you simply "came home from a real hard day."

Marsha Norman's *Getting Out*, a play about a young woman beginning life again after a prison sentence, unfolds in this environment:

> Both acts are set in a dingy one-room apartment. There is a twin bed and one chair, but no other furniture. There is a sink, an apartment-size combination stove and refrigerator and a counter with cabinets above. Dirty curtains conceal the bars on the outside of the single window. . . . A catwalk stretches above the apartment and several cell areas connect to it by stairways. An apron downstage completes the enclosure of the apartment in playing areas for the past.

Norman uses fewer modifiers than Miller; the only descriptive word is *dingy*. Nevertheless, there is enough information for skilled actors to discern the weighty atmosphere. Her recent past is oppressive, as her new home is surrounded onstage by catwalks and jail cells. Even the windows of her new urban apartment have bars on them. And there is a feeling of solitary confinement as suggested by the "twin bed and one chair, but no other furniture." Your rehearsal space will probably be spacious, brightly lit, and well populated by cast, director, and others. If you rehearse your actions in that environment without embracing the atmospheric mood Norman gives you, no audience will believe you are living in the character's space created by the designers.

The fountain angel in Williams' *Summer and Smoke*, the rolling farmland and magical sunlight in *Finian's Rainbow*, the decadent furnishings in Christopher Hampton's *Les Liaisons Dangereuse*, the mechanized whirrs and buzzes of Sophie Treadwell's *Machinal*—each help create an atmosphere shared by both actor and audience. And both will respond to this atmosphere through unconscious, emotional connection.

Humor

The truth is like castor oil, it is bitter to swallow
and people don't want it; so, you make them laugh
and when their mouths are open, you pour it in.
HAROLD CLURMAN

Laughter is a purely emotional experience and an easy way to reach the audience's heart. Not counting those recovering from surgery, who *doesn't* like to laugh? Humor is one of the quickest ways to get an audience to love a character. Used well, it can make a difficult message easy to swallow. It can heighten tragedy through contrast. It can clarify complexity. Laughter is only now being documented as enormously powerful in health, memory, and longevity. What better way to reach the heart than through a good guffaw?

Neil Simon often addresses the subject of uncompromising incompatibility. When people are obsessed with a singular point of view without respect for another's, unnecessary violence and isolation result. Yet he uses humor to make this point. In *The Sunshine Boys*, the two battling generals are former vaudeville partners reunited for a television retrospective. One is emotionally unpredictable and volatile; the other is sensibly controlled and articulate—heart versus head. Needless to say, watching these doddering men is hysterical, but the point is made as we see ourselves in them. *The Odd Couple* approaches this topic by using two divorced men each trying to change, rather than accept, the other. *Barefoot in the Park* was written in the sixties when all traditional thinking was being challenged by a new generation, and the "generation gap" was a common subject in newspapers and magazines. Simon embodied this in two newlyweds, one spontaneously carefree, and the other methodically controlled. The conflict is mirrored again in the wife's mother who "sleeps on a board" and her date, an aging hippie who "sleeps on the floor."

Simon's conflicts parallel Democrat versus Republican, traditional versus experimental, communist versus capitalist—and takes them out of our intellects. Once we laugh, we can safely recognize the similarity in our differences.

Humor is an easy doorway to the heart. Once you're in, you can touch it deeply. If you want to make your audience cry, make them laugh first.

Poetry

Since the Greeks, poetry has been used to open the heart. Shakespeare did not write 154 love "essays." Beauty always reaches the heart; "love at first sight" is evidence of that. And the beauty of language composed less for straightforward clarity than for the beauty of its sounds and images reaches the heart in the same way.

When Juliet awaits the eve of her wedding night to Romeo, she pleads:

> Come, gentle night, come, loving, black-brow'd night,
> Give me my Romeo, and, when I shall die,
> Take him and cut him out in little stars,
> And he will make the face of heaven soften
> That all the world will be in love with night,
> And pay no worship to the garish sun.

Not bad for a thirteen-year-old.

Poetry can also boost mild humor into hysterical comedy. In Stephen Sondheim's *West Side Story*, the gang members act out a mock trial in the song "Gee, Officer Krupke." If the lines were prose—"I was an unwanted pregnancy, my schoolteachers have no use for me, and my parents wouldn't even share their marijuana with me"—it would not be nearly as funny as the quick-rhythmed, rhyming couplets of the song. The lyrics are also an excellent example of how a difficult topic can be addressed acceptably through humor; the buck-passing futile efforts of government in helping inner-city youth is acted out through playful ridicule.

Musical theatre relies heavily on poetry in song lyric as well as music (see Part III of this chapter) to create its highly emotional effects.

Metaphor

The unique way one person experiences an emotion is one of the greatest challenges artists have had to communicate. Can you ever *know* exactly what one person feels when they say, "I love you"? We know what love means to ourselves, and there is a recognizable commonality to it, but there are also subtle nuances that are distinctive and even peculiar to each person. We have all felt pain and loss to some degree, but how do the parents feel who have outlived their children? Suppose a writer wants an audience to know exactly what he or she feels about . . . anything. An audience cannot "try on" the author's heart and see how it feels. What can they do?

Describe music for someone who has never heard sound. You could look it up in a dictionary: "The art of organizing tones to produce a coherent sequence of sounds intended to elicit an aesthetic response in a listener." Is that accurate? Yes. Is it music? No. Language only offers an intellectual understanding of music, an art form that must be experienced. But you could use a parallel. Is music like painting? Like food? Like a massage? It depends on what music is for you and what painting, food, or massage are for the deaf person.

In Anna Hamilton Phelan's screenplay for *Mask*, a boy tries to explain red, blue, and billowy (as in clouds) to a girl who has been blind since birth. Since she has no *familiar* reference, it is impossible for him until he comes up with an idea: He places a rock in hot water and another in the freezer. He hands her the hot rock and says, "This is red. When it cools it will be yellow." About the cold rock he says, "This is blue, and when it warms up, it will be green." He places puffed cotton batting in her hands and identifies it as "billowy." Finally, she begins to understand.

But what did he do? He used the sense of touch and temperature that she did have, in order to help her understand the sense of sight and color that she did not. This is basically the definition for *metaphor*: use of the familiar to clarify the unfamiliar. All fiction is metaphor. A novel tells a story that you know is fantasy, not fact, but that you recognize as true to reality. "This is like that" is how imagery, metaphor, and simile communicate.

If playwrights want their deeply personal, abstract feelings to reach yours, they can do so by creating a metaphoric parallel common to a greater variety of people. The torturous frustration of being in love with a man who cannot love you back is *like* being a cat on a hot tin roof—tautly frantic and jittery but too frightened to jump off.

The trouble is, we become less and less able to "metaphorize" as we become more entrenched in technology, finance, and science. Metaphor is worthless in these arenas. How often do you see the selling point "based on a true story"? *Everything* is "based" on a true story; Peter Shaffer read a one-paragraph news item that inspired him to write *Equus*. Does that mean the entire play is "based on a true story"? Fiction requires compassion for a truth parallel to reality. But as people become desensitized by the barrage of common violence, news, and graphic documentary, parallel truth pales no matter how rich. (If the general population were as adept at metaphor as actors are, they would be less easily manipulated by the use of them in advertising and politics.) Time, voices, and music have become digital. If something cannot be measured, explained, or enumerated then it does not exist. Money and votes are measurable; dignity and integrity are not.

But metaphor is crucial for artists. Artists must convey the immeasurable, the unexplainable, and the innumerable that enrich a culture and are the subject of fine plays. Even if the contemporary world in which an actor lives prioritizes the scientific approach, actors must embrace the history of civilization and *all* that it has contributed. If you want to reach your audience's heart, you cannot do it through their minds.

Metaphor in Titles Titles often contain metaphors for the script's heart. Many of Tennessee Williams' plays have metaphorical titles. Laura's glass menagerie in his play of the same name is a metaphor for the fragility, isolation, and vulnerability of its characters. Enid Bagnold used a "chalk garden" in her play of the same title to metaphorize the loveless atmosphere in which children are being raised; how healthy can things grow in a garden whose soil is mostly chalk? August Strindberg entitled his play *Dance of Death* to metaphorize a mutually torturous and fatal marriage. *Children of a Lesser God, The Seagull, The Prisoner of 2nd Avenue, The Little Foxes, The Effect of Gamma Rays on Man-in-the-Moon Marigolds*—each are metaphors for the script's deeper statements.

Metaphor Through Symbols Throughout a script there may be other images that are of more use to production designers than to actors. Nevertheless, an actor should be aware of them in order to understand the script's heart. Repeated references, direct and indirect, to "eyes" and "sight" are used throughout *King Lear*. Fear of the unknown and safety are represented by darkness and light in Inge's *The Dark at the Top of the Stairs*. The moon as a metaphor for mystery, magic, and romance enhances many plays such as *A Midsummer Night's Dream*, LaPine's *Twelve Dreams*, and O'Neill's *A Moon for the Misbegotten*. Although you cannot play these symbols, a thorough understanding of what they represent will help you in your understanding of the script and the function of your character within it.

Metaphor Through Character The character's function within a script serves as a metaphor for universal human or societal aspects. Character names often reflect this.

Williams' *Hello, From Bertha* is about a prostitute, Bertha, dying from a venereal disease and Goldie, the madam who needs the room vacated for clients. Bertha contracted her fatal illness working for Goldie, whose only concern is the amount of money she loses every minute her room is unavailable. She cannot call the police or the hospital (not very good P.R. to have a squad car or ambulance parked outside a brothel) and must compel Bertha to leave on her own.

Goldie represents commerce, the cold-hearted automatons who only concern themselves with the "bottom line." Aptly, she is named after the metal used for centuries as currency. Bertha represents the hardworking human powerless against exploitative business. No wonder her name sounds like the very beginning of life. Yet, some actors play Goldie as genuinely sympathetic, and so the conflict becomes Bertha and Goldie *against* random adversity. Those actors must weave elaborate and exhausting rationalizations to make sense of that choice because the dialogue and actions really don't support it. If they simply examined the clear metaphors Williams offers, they'd find a much stronger interpretation, and an easier one to pull off.

The two couples of Edward Albee's *Who's Afraid of Virginia Woolf?* are named George and Martha, and Nick and Honey. Characters in Alice Childress' *The Wine in the Wilderness* include Oldtimer, Sonny-man, and Tomorrow. Restoration theatre is replete with obvious character names: Sir Anthony Absolute, Mr. Pinchwife and Mr. Homer, Lady Wishfort, and the most famous, Mrs. Malaprop, whose name has become a noun—*malapropism.*

Metaphor Within Dialogue The specific lyrical metaphors of language make little *logical* sense. Love does not "make the world go 'round"; the gravitational pull of the sun creates orbital tension—you know the rest. But emotionally, they are totally clear. Metaphors take language, a tool of the mind, and poeticize it into a tool of the heart.

Metaphoric language is not some alien device used only by old-fashioned poets and overly dramatic divas. It exists in our current technological society. Standup comedians use metaphors often. "She was the nun from hell." "He has the brains of a wide-mouthed bass." "My head looks like a bowling ball with hair." Rap music lyrics use metaphors extensively, such as when Craig Mack says he is going to "kick a new flava [flavor] in your ear." What he is saying is that he is "going to introduce a sound so new that it will first shock you before you savor its fresh nuances." But which image conveys the truth of the idea more totally, concisely, and captivatingly?

You use metaphors yourself. Describe a bizarre nightmare: "I was walking through, like, lime Jell-O but it had big waves like Maui." Or a peculiar pain: "It feels like a piano is sitting on my lungs whenever I inhale." Or what it feels like to end a relationship: "When he said good-bye, I felt like a giant cookie cutter punched a hole in my chest." As we speak, we speak from the mind until we get to an experience that cannot be expressed through literal language. "I thought it was really, really, really, REALLY funny" just doesn't do the same as "I laughed so hard my stomach fell out."

The dialogue in Tennessee Williams' *A Streetcar Named Desire* explains its central metaphor. Blanche Dubois' sister Stella tries to communicate the intangible bond she has for Stanley:

> STELLA: But there are things that happen between a man and a woman in the dark—that sort of make everything else seem—unimportant. *(Pause.)*
> BLANCHE: What you are talking about is brutal desire—just— Desire!—the name of that rattle-trap streetcar that bangs through the quarter, up one old narrow street and down another . . .
> STELLA: Haven't you ever ridden on that streetcar?
> BLANCHE: It brought me here.—Where I'm not wanted and where I'm ashamed to be.

To play Stella's lines, you have to understand why that mode of public transportation becomes a metaphor for marital passion. What better way to describe that relationship than the roller-coasterlike adventure of a rickety streetcar that could run away and crash into a wall at any moment? Stella's adventure is animalistic and base to Blanche. The pause before Blanche's response suggests that Blanche knows exactly what she is talking about; the difference is that she rejects that level of existence even though it is a haunting presence in her body.

Lyrical language has different energy than natural conversation. All shifts in energy require transitions. When the mind is unable to express an idea, the heart struggles for the familiar parallel. This takes effort. Few people are as spontaneously lyrical as they look on paper. You will be amazed at how much more natural your metaphoric dialogue will feel if you take a moment to struggle for the exact expression from the heart. It can make the difference between artificial dialogue and heartfelt expression. Therefore, it is crucial to understand when characters are choosing to speak metaphorically—from the heart—and when they are speaking literally—from the mind.

The most famous monologue in *A Streetcar Named Desire* is referred to by people in theatre as "the candle monologue." This is because the atmosphere of the scene, the scene's heart, is metaphorized in the single burning candle Blanche lights. Tell a professional you are working on Williams' "candle monologue" and they will know which play you are rehearsing.

In the speech, Blanche attempts to reveal her true soul to Mitch, a suitor. She speaks of her unique experience of love, her marriage, her guilt, and the resulting ruins. Let's break down the speech into its literal and metaphorical elements:

> BLANCHE: I loved someone, too, and the person I loved I lost.
> MITCH: Dead? A man?
> BLANCHE: He was a boy, just a boy, when I was a very young girl.

This is the first metaphor. She is speaking of her first husband. Was he literally "a boy"? What does "a boy" and "a very young girl" literally mean to you? Twelve years old? Five? Certainly, they must have been adult enough to marry. But the heart recognizes that this is only half true. He was not a man but had the soul of a child when she was still a child herself. When Mitch asks, "A man?" the literal answer is "yes," but Blanche's heart knows that the literal answer is not the honest answer. If the actress playing her takes merely a moment to search for the whole truth, Blanche's response, "He was . . . a boy" will feel more honest and natural.

> I was sixteen when I made the discovery—love. All at once and much, much too completely.

Although she is expressing her experience poetically, it is still a literal statement. "Discovery" might be metaphoric, and that is an equally valid interpretation.

> It was like you suddenly turned a blinding light on something that had always been half in shadow.

This is a perfect example of how Williams conveys Blanche's unique personal experience of falling in love for the first time to an audience who have their own unique experiences of first falling in love. Using the familiar images of "blinding light" and "half shadows," he is able to illustrate the night-and-day change and the sudden clarity it made in Blanche's life.

> That's how it struck the world for me. But I was unlucky. Deluded. There was something different about the boy, a nervousness, a softness and tenderness which wasn't like a man's, although he wasn't the least bit effeminate looking—

This is highly descriptive, but each idea is an attempt to describe literally what she experienced in him.

> —still—that thing was there.

As blah as "that thing" is, the word itself becomes a metaphor for the indescribable. *Thing* is a stand-in for any unknown. *Thing* conjures all the alien fears we have lurking under our beds. She speaks of a *quality* he had, but, to her, it was so intangible and mysterious that she was reduced to using the word *thing*.

> He came to me for help. I didn't know that. I didn't find out anything till after our marriage when we had run away and come back . . .

This is either literal or metaphoric. If you choose that Blanche eloped with her first husband, then they literally ran off and then came home. Personally, I believe that Blanche, having been raised the elder daughter on an aristocratic plantation, had a spectacular wedding. In this case, the "run away and come back" is a metaphor for the whirlwind of excitement and passion that surrounded her wedding. Or it could simply refer to the honeymoon.

> . . . and all I knew was I'd failed him in some mysterious way and was not able to give the help he needed but couldn't speak of!

Literal.

> He was in the quicksands and clutching me—but I wasn't holding him out, I was slipping in with him!

(I don't need to point this one out, do I?)

> I didn't know that. I didn't know anything except I loved him un-
> endurably . . .

"Unendurably" borders on metaphor. Your interpretation.

> . . . but without being able to help him or help myself. Then I
> found out. In the worst of all possible ways. By coming into a
> room that I thought was empty—which wasn't empty, but had
> two people in it . . . the boy I had married and an older man who
> had been his friend for years.

Try not to confuse lyrical rhythms and the beauty of well-placed
sounds and words as metaphor. The above is literal.

> Afterwards, we pretended that nothing had been discovered. Yes,
> the three of us drove out to Moon Lake Casino . . .

"Moon Lake Casino" might be a metaphor in a literature class, but
for the character, it is the literal name of the place they went.

> . . . very drunk and laughing all the way. We danced the Varsou-
> viana! Suddenly, in the middle of the dance the boy I had married
> broke away from me and ran out of the casino.

Notice there have been no metaphors for quite some time. As
Shakespeare used poetry for his heightened emotions and characters, and prose for the more common, Williams does not grace the
ugliness of what Blanche is describing with the beauty of metaphor.
For the character, perhaps it is so painful, she cannot bear to speak
through her heart.

> A few moments later—a shot.

This is when the onomatopoeic sound of the word metaphorizes
the sudden and harsh shock of the gunfire. The literal narrative
would be, "A few moments later, there was a shot." Or "I heard a
shot" or "A shot rang out." Say the word out loud and hear how
well it communicates a moment: Suddenly—a **shot**.

> I ran out—all did!—all ran and gathered about the terrible thing at the edge of the lake! I couldn't get near for the crowding. Then somebody caught my arm. "Don't go any closer! Come back! You don't want to see!" See? See what!

Here too, the quoted dialogue without the "he said" or "I said" echoes the chaos.

> Then I heard voices say—Allan! Allan! The Grey boy! He'd stuck a revolver into his mouth, and fired—so that the back of his head had been—blown away!

So far, the monologue has been told in linear sequence until:

> It was because—on the dance-floor—unable to stop myself—I'd suddenly said—"I saw! I know! You disgust me . . ."

Only here does she backtrack and fill in the missing piece—her responsibility for his violent suicide. But that also means that when Blanche gets to the chronological point for this moment, she intentionally skips it. That point would come between "Varsouviana" and "Suddenly in the middle of the dance floor." The precise moment Blanche chooses to eliminate this most painful guilt from her story to Mitch must be chosen and filled with action.

> And then the searchlight which had been turned on the world was turned off again and never for one moment since has there been any light stronger than this—kitchen—candle . . .

The monologue returns to its metaphoric image. Listen to the sound and power evoked by *searchlight* in contrast to the mundane image and clicking sound of *kitchen candle*.

This is metaphor and lyricism at its heart-reaching best. Few playwrights have had the compassion for humanity that Tennessee Williams had. When the rest of the world might have laughed or looked down upon the mentally unbalanced, sexually deviate, or financially destitute, Williams opened his heart to them. How else but with his gifts for metaphor, atmosphere, poetry, and storytelling could he infect audience's hearts with the abstract but infinite compassion in his?

Part III: Reaching the Crowd

We probably owe our profession to a clever water buffalo.

Quite some time ago, a hunter returned victorious with enough food to feed his entire starving community. After days of stalking a particularly elusive water buffalo, speed and agility had proven the hunter's superiority on the food chain. The chase had been dangerous, thrilling, and dramatic. Too bad the entire tribe couldn't be there to watch. After everyone stuffs themselves on buffalo burgers, the hunter relates the story of the kill. The full-bellied tribe listens awestruck as their hero reenacts the event, embellishing a bit here and there for effect, acting out his fear against the angry animal's spirit. Its clever eyes, his courageous feats, its powerful limbs, his agile maneuvers. Portraying the beast, he charges directly at one tribesman who leaps backward and screams. The others laugh. As the hunter finally throws the fatal spear, he howls his doomed prey's death cry. He falls to the ground and his audience leaps up, yells, and celebrates. They have become part of the event.

From its beginnings in prehistoric humanity, theatre has always *directly* involved the audience. Even tribal religious ritual—another source of theatre—involved *all* community members through dance, percussion, and chant. The ancient Greek *rhapsodes* (poets who recited their epic poems) performed their works directly for and to their audiences. The Greek choruses represented and led the audience much like a pastor leads a congregation. Roman, Elizabethan, Commedia, Restoration, melodrama—all *used* their audiences as direct or indirect parts of the show. In fact, from Shakespeare's time to the late eighteenth century, some members of the audience actually sat *on* the stage.

It was only during the nineteenth century when Ibsen and Strindberg began redefining theatre that audiences became passive and separate observers. Psychological Realism was created as the glories of the individual's mind and spirit were being valued above the blind acceptance of social and religious convention. So in order to re-create a believable, recognizable reality, the audience had to disappear into the dark and peer through an imaginary "fourth wall" like bold voyeurs.

The invention of Psychological Realism made motion pictures as theatre possible. Audiences were already primed to watch passively in the dark in exchange for being privy to highly personal moments.

Television continued this but brought that privacy into our homes. In the last hundred years, the collaboration of audience with the theatre event has most often been suppressed in favor of fourth-wall Realism. But film can create intimacy and psychological vulnerability much more effectively than the stage; you can't get right into someone's face and read their eyes when watching theatre. But with film, everyone gets a seat close enough to see subtle facial expressions. Because media does this particular style best and is far more readily available, the popularity of live theatre has fallen in comparison.

But what does theatre have that films do not? *Unison, immediacy,* and *transitory singularity.* There is no detachment between actor and audience, no partition between film and flesh. What the audience watches is there *now;* what they hear is what the actors hear, what they sense is what the actors sense, and all responses are immediate. A major part of that sensory involvement originates in the crowd's energy. Anyone who has performed for a time can describe the "feel" of a Saturday night audience in contrast to a Wednesday matinee. During the Gulf War, many actors spoke of the tension they could feel in the audience and how the performance was influenced. That audience energy is the final ingredient of the show. Unlike a film, every performance is subtly transmuted through the unique combination of people involved: actors and audience. This combination has never joined forces before. It will never join forces again.

The doorway that playwrights who reach the crowd use is through the body. When an entire audience laughs or startles in unison, sways to the rhythm of music, or spontaneously answers when a character solicits their opinion, a physical experience becomes the connecting doorway. These are the hardest plays to convert to film successfully. But it is that kind of theatre—theatre that has existed as part of human nature since tribal living—that people are hungry for. Look at the sudden success of "interactive media." Look at the proliferation of stand-up comedy in clubs and television. There is no fourth wall in stand-up. They contact the audience *directly*—sometimes physically. Look at the continued success of musical theatre, which nearly always opens the fourth wall and directly reaches the toe-tapping crowd. The loud and passionate crowds of sports events in massive stadiums echo the energy and size of the ancient audiences at Greek Dionysian festivals in enormous amphitheaters.

Many techniques of modern crowd-reaching plays were discovered in classic theatre, when the audience was always involved. However, since 90 percent of the acting that today's actors have come in contact with has been from television or film, they often play these moments like artificial theatrical devices. Sincere *contact* with the audience must be made for crowd-reaching plays to succeed. Even though most modern theatres keep the audience in the dark and the actors brightly lit (if in performance you can see past the third row you're lucky), you can still sense their energy, connect with their attention, and speak to them as though they were with you. This is when the astounding and unique powers of theatre create magic.

Opening the Fourth Wall

Direct Address From the hunter around the fire to Aeschylus' Prometheus to Rabbi Chemelwitz in Tony Kushner's *Angels in America*, directly addressing the audience has been a surefire way to reach them. Even if we don't believe the actors see *us-as-individual*, we know they see *us-as-collective* and the perceived eye contact makes a tangible connection.

The prologue (see Chapter 1) was the first and most common form of direct address. The speaker excites the audience about the subject and events of the ensuing play like a circus barker pulling people into a tent. Or like the red-light district welcome wagon outside strip shows: "Wait 'til you see the lovely beauties we have inside. . . ."

The prologue speaker is either a character from the play, the chorus leader, or a perimeter figure created for that purpose. The audience is spoken to directly. But as theatre has evolved over centuries, audiences can represent people in the speaking character's life. In Peter Nichols' *A Day in the Death of Joe Egg*, the audience first represents Brian's classroom of students. The opening:

> BRI: That's enough! (*He pauses, then almost at once shouts louder*) I
> said enough! (*He pauses, **staring at the audience***) Another
> word and you'll all be here til five o'clock . . . I didn't even get
> to the end of the corridor before there was such a din all the
> other teachers started opening their doors as much as to say
> "what the hell's going on"—there's SOMEBODY TALKING
> NOW! . . .

When the story proceeds into Brian and Sheila's home, we become visiting guests. The play continues—sometimes oblivious of us, and other times directly including us.

> BRI: What are you telling them?
> SHEILA: What?
> BRI: I heard you talking. (*Sheila picks a thread from her clothes.*) I heard you mention Joe. (*Sheila does not answer.* **To audience**) Sheila's got a theory about Joe's birth. She doesn't blame the doctors. She blames herself.
> SHEILA: I don't say that. I say it wasn't entirely the doctors.
> BRI: It was because she choked back.
> SHEILA: It was partly that.
> BRI: Because she slept around.
> SHEILA: I think it was partly because I'd been promiscuous, yes, and my subconscious was making me shrink or withdraw from motherhood, all right!
> (*Pause. Bri looks away. Sheila goes on sprucing.*)
> BRI: That vicar said it was the devil's doing. Why don't you believe that? It's about as brilliant.
> SHEILA (*Shrugging*): It comes down in the end to what you believe.
> BRI: I'll tell you what I believe.
> SHEILA: I know what you believe.
> BRI (**Pointing at the audience**): They don't. (**To the audience**) I believe the doctor botched it. There was no other cause. (*To Sheila*) That specialist said as much, he said it had nothing to do with the way you lived.

The scene continues as we bounce from passive spectators to silent participants.

Most important when playing these scenes, you must know who you are talking to. Sometimes, like in *Volpone*, it simply is "the audience." This is usually when the play has a presentational style—as in classic theatre; a musical review; a one-person biography, such as *The Last of the Belles* (about Emily Dickenson); or plays about performers, such as John Osborne's *The Entertainer*. In Nichols' play, we might represent the world's "social judges" who act as friends and guests but pass judgment so strongly that they make the characters second-guess their own conclusions. In Peter Shaffer's *Equus*, the doctor might be speaking to a medical jury board, or structured society, or all his former patients:

> DR. DYSART (*He steps out of the square and walks around the upstage end of it,* **storming at the audience**): I'll heal the rash on his body. I'll erase the welts cut into him by flaying manes. When that's done, I'll set him on a nice mini-scooter and send him puttering off into the Normal world where animals are treated properly: made extinct, or put into servitude, or tethered beside them—blinking our nights away in a nonstop drench of cathode ray over our shriveling heads!

There are rarely "definitive" choices about whom that audience is; the actor creates an identity that works best for him or her. But the actor who nonspecifically speaks "out" without creating the "who *they* are" builds a stronger fourth wall than the one he or she is trying to break open; the audience does not feel included but senses being spoken "at." The actor who creates the audience as real people who are an important part of the play has the unique power of live theatre that electrifies performance.

The Aside The technique in *A Day in the Death of Joe Egg* of flip-flopping the audience from passivity to activity is an evolution of the *aside*, which was already used for centuries in classic drama. An aside is when the character steps "aside" the action and speaks directly to the audience for a brief comment. Traditionally, the hand masks the face away from the other characters so that they are not privy to this private interaction. It provides an intimate point of view that only the actor and the audience share, which would otherwise be impossible within the play's circumstances.

As Dorine watches two young lovers fight over a misunderstanding in Molière's *Tartuffe*, she includes the audience with her amusement:

> MARIANNE: To give it [hostile advice] didn't cause your heart to break.
> VALERE: I gave it, Madam, only for your sake.
> MARIANNE: And it's for your sake that I take it, Sir.
> DORINE (**Withdrawing to the rear of the stage**): Let's see which fool will prove the stubborner.

With Dorine's invitation, we do not watch from afar; we join her as a member of the household enjoying this foolish exchange.

The aside can also provide an insight into a character that is not normally revealed publicly. In Oscar Wilde's *The Importance of Being Earnest*, two rivals share afternoon tea:

CECILY: May I offer you some tea, Miss Fairfax?
MISS FAIRFAX (*With elaborate politeness*): Thank you (**Aside.**)
　　Detestable girl! But I require tea!

As the characters wear their masks of civility, we get to see the drag-ons behind the lace.

The audience can be drafted into coconspiracy. This involves us more as we become silent accomplices. In Wycherly's *The Country Wife*, Fidget introduces his wife to Homer, whom he believes to be impotent with women.

FIDGET: Won't you be acquainted with her sir?—(**Aside**) So, the
　　report is true, I find, by his coldness or aversion to the sex;
　　but I'll play the wag with him.—Pray salute my wife, my lady,
　　sir.
HORNER: I will kiss no man's wife, sire, for him, sir; I have taken
　　my eternal leave, sir, of the sex already, sir.
FIDGET: (**Aside**) Ha, ha, ha, I'll plague him yet.

Remember, when the aside was invented the audience was illumi-nated, the classes were separated, and you knew which sections of the audience were on "your character's team." The playing of the two worlds simultaneously (the play's scene and the audience's in-volvement) is much like two tough guys posturing before a fight:

TOUGH GUY 1: Oh yeah?
TOUGH GUY 2: Yeah!
BUDDIES OF TOUGH GUY 2: You tell 'em, Tough Guy 2!
TOUGH GUY 1: Yeah? Well, I'll "yeah" YOU down your throat!
BUDDIES OF TOUGH GUY 1: Yeah, down your throat!
TOUGH GUY 1 (*Does a high-five with his BUDDIES*): Down his
　　throat!!!
BUDDIES OF TOUGH GUY 2 (*To TOUGH GUY 2*): You gonna let him
　　talk to you like that?
TOUGH GUY 2 (*To his BUDDIES*): The heck I am! (*To TOUGH
　　GUY 1*) Down MY throat? I'll "yeah" you down YOUR throat!
BUDDIES OF TOUGH GUY 2: Yeah!
TOUGH GUY 2 (*To BUDDIES*): Yeah!!!

You get the idea . . .

The point is, whether you're picking a fight in front of your buddies, getting up the nerve to ask someone out while your pals encourage from a safe distance, or reading a book to children while engaging them simultaneously through relevant questions, playing two scenes at once is common and natural. This is when the aside and other forms of opening the fourth wall work.

Audience Involvement In the 1960s and '70s, theatre recognized that film and television excelled at Psychological Realism and rather than compete with it through massive "special effects" (which are popular today), reexplored the uniqueness of live performance. Experimental theatre often included "audience participation." Actors often emerged from the house, or left the stage to speak or sit with audience members. The performance space expanded past the stage into the aisles and sometimes into the street. One play I went to had the audience led by hand into dark rooms while slices of pineapple were gently placed in surprised mouths. This was an attempt to rediscover the audience involvement that was lost with Psychological Realism.

But audiences have changed in the past couple of centuries. We have moved from extended to nuclear to one-parent families. We are less trusting of strangers who want to stick something in our mouths, or even speak to us in person. When we see a play, we are less open to leaving our safe passivity to become part of the performance. So the experiments in audience participation were largely abandoned to informal shows by magicians, hypnotists, and comics.

Nevertheless, audience involvement from acceptably safe distances (defined by current societies) is theatre's strongest asset, and a large variety of successful genres are being created. Performance art is one example. Jim Cartwright's *Road* had the audience seated among the actors who involved the audience but did not require them to participate. *A Chorus Line* placed the casting choreographer at the back of the theatre so that the auditioning dancers spoke to us as much as to him. *The Mystery of Edwin Drood*, based on the unfinished Dickens novel, halts the play where the novel stops. The audience is then solicited for the "best" ending, which is voted upon and then performed.

Another relatively new form of theatre takes place in alternate locations where the audience literally becomes part of the show (although their actual participation is left up to them). *Tamara* is performed in a Tudor mansion. All scenes transpire simultaneously in its different rooms. The audience, houseguests who sup with the characters at intermission, can choose to stay in one room as people come and go, follow a character of their choice through one plot line, or haphazardly wander around stumbling on events. The play is different for each individual and can be seen many times without repetition.

Tony 'n Tina's Wedding follows the nuptial day of an Italian working-class couple. The audience members become the wedding guests and are occasionally accosted, "Wha, so this is how you dress for a wedding, you pig!" *Bernie's Bar Mitzvah* and *Grandma Sylvia's Funeral* are variations on that theme. Murder-mystery plays take place on trains, cruise ships, and in resorts, where the actors and audience merge so that you don't know if the people you're sitting across from are actors or really a funny-looking couple from Scarsdale. Actors in these plays have strong improvisational backgrounds because spontaneity and instant connection to an unpredictable partner—the audience—is crucial.

Guerrilla Theatre, named after the soldiers who infiltrate the enemy by masquerading as one of them, has been performed primarily in South America and less-privileged countries. In this type of play that reaches the crowd, the actors pretend to be shoppers, or police, or virtually any recognizable person and begin acting their scenes as though they were genuine events. The surrounding crowd believes and participates as though it were reality; they have been abducted into attending a play.

"Site-specific" plays—plays that take place in a bar if the setting is a bar or in a hospital if the setting is a hospital—attempt to involve an audience by changing their environment. Without a traditional theatre, spectators abandon the conditioned reflex to remain quiet and passive in a theatre seat.

The reinvention of audience involvement is still in its experimental stages, but when it works and the actors genuinely make contact—literal or figurative—with an audience of strangers, a magnificent experience is created each night, and for *only* one night.

Music Musical theatre enters two doorways: heart and body. The poetry of the song lyric and emotional subject matter reach the heart. The music reaches the body. Before anything else is the mother's heartbeat. What follows is the movement of the body and finally the expression of the voice. Music began with percussion, probably sticks and hollow logs, but its influence on the body was ingrained in the womb.

The abstraction of musical sound communicates to the body to relax, or become frightened, or move, and so on. There is no logic to this; it is an intuitive response that is more marked in our species than in any other. If you've ever had "that tune running over and over" in your head, you know the illogical yet tenacious invasion of music in your body. How easy is it to sit still at a dance club or rock concert? Chirping crickets instruct our bodies to relax for the night. Crackling thunder warns us to take cover. Through this physical response, playwrights can reach the heart and crowd through shared atmosphere. Williams' *A Streetcar Named Desire* describes:

> *In this part of New Orleans you are practically always just around the corner, or a few doors down the street, from a tinny piano being played with the infatuated fluency of brown fingers. This "blue piano" expresses the spirit of the life which goes on here.*

Like an accelerating heartbeat, the pulsing music in Weber's *The Phantom of the Opera* alerts anxiety in the crowd. The opening musical phrase of "Over the Rainbow" feels like a deep, lonely sigh. The revolutionary march song "Can You Hear the People Sing" from *Les Misérables* impels us with its steady boot-stepping beats. Each reaches the body first through the sense of hearing and triggers physical response.

The percussive beats in music can accomplish the same thing in dialogue. David Mamet uses overlapping dialogue and unfinished sentences in sharp snippets to heighten the mounting tension of *Oleanna's* climactic scene. Here, a professor attempts to appease a student who is pressing sexual harassment charges:

CAROL: All right. I have a list.
JOHN: . . . a list.
CAROL: Here is a list of books, which we . . .
JOHN: . . . a list of books . . . ?
CAROL: That's right. Which we find questionable.
JOHN: What?
CAROL: Is this so bizarre . . . ?
JOHN: I can't believe . . .
CAROL: It's not necessary that you believe it.
JOHN: Academic freedom . . .
CAROL: Someone chooses the books. If you can choose them, others can. What are you, "God"?
JOHN: . . . no, no, the "dangerous."

CAROL: You have an agenda, we have an agenda. I am not
interested in your feelings or your motivation, but your
actions. If you would like me to speak to the Tenure
Committee, here is my list. You are a Free Person, you decide.
(*Pause*)
JOHN: Give me the list. (*She does so. He reads.*)
CAROL: I think you'll find . . .
JOHN: I'm capable of reading it. Thank you.
CAROL: We have a number of texts we need re . . .
JOHN: I see that.
CAROL: We're amenable to . . .
JOHN: Aha. Well, let me look over the . . .
CAROL: I think that . . .
JOHN: LOOK, I'm reading your demands. All right!?

The tense rhythm is felt first in the body even before the mind can
register the ideas being argued. The sounds of the language itself
become music. The inherent theatricality of music is discussed further in the next chapter.

Other Tricks That Work Startling someone is a good way to get their
attention. Killers leaping out of the woodwork, guns going off, dead
bodies falling out of closets—all these provoke a spontaneous physical and vocal response in the audience. Naked bodies are a pretty
sure way of creating physical reactions. Darkness forces an audience
to peer harder. Silence forces us to listen. Hearty laughter can be infectious. Sound effects can provoke relaxation, anxiety, laughter,
alertness, and an infinite amount of physical responses.

In fact, nearly anything in theatre that provokes physical response is innately theatrical. The next chapter discusses theatricality in detail.

9 The Architecture of Theatricality

Unlike anything read, a script is performed to an audience. This audience, unlike readers, participates in a location not of their choosing, at a time not of their choosing. If they misunderstand a moment or they are momentarily distracted, they cannot reread the paragraph or stand up to ask the actors, "I'm sorry, I was thinking about something else, would you mind doing that part over again?" They cannot eat, drink, stretch, or use the bathroom. They have no control over the pace to ponder or absorb a given detail. They sit in relatively uncomfortable seats, often next to some stranger who has the ridiculous notion that the armrest is for them. Essentially, every audience is a "captive" audience.

Therefore, playwrights have developed techniques that grab an audience's attention, focus them on crucial details, and keep their concentrations engaged enough to forget the discomfort of being held captive in a theatre space, as well as life's incessant distractions. Notice during intermission how people crane their necks, rub their backs, and bolt to the rest rooms; it is only during this break that they become aware of their discomfort. Notice how during a good play or movie you have temporarily forgotten about your day job's stress, your lover's demands, or the unopened letter from the I.R.S. Theatricality does this.

Theatricality is "dramatic charisma." It is the elements that latch onto the audience's attention and evoke their empathic response in heart, mind, and/or body. All artistic expression attempts to involve its audience and elicit response. Painters evoke response through color, shape, light, and composition. Musicians trigger reactions through sounds and rhythms. Novelists stimulate the imagination through words, stories, imagery, characters, and poetry. Playwrights reach their audience through theatrical *actions*. Although theatre borrows communicative techniques from all the arts, pure theatricality communicates through action. In the following section some of the many active elements that make theatre theatrical are explored.

Beams, Struts, and Bolts

Spectacle

In the years around three hundred B.C., even Aristotle recognized how crucial the visual is to effective drama. Universally, in all languages, we go to see a play. We may "hear" a reading or "watch" television, but we SEE a play. *Seventy percent of all synaptic responses in the brain originate in the retinas of the eyes;* that's how important the visual is to our species. What we see onstage has the strongest potential of immediate audience involvement. One of the first theatrical spectacles was the *deus ex machina*, which literally means "god from machine." In ancient Greek times, elaborate machines, cranes, and pulleys were built to visually represent the power and magnificence of divine intervention. After Medea exacts her revenge:

> *There is a rumbling sound, and out of a cloud above the house, Medea appears in a chariot drawn by dragons. By her side are the dead bodies of the two boys Medea, with a cold, vindictive smile, whisks away in the chariot.*

Even by today's jaded standards of computer-generated images and astounding technological skill, that dramatic spectacle provokes gasps. This is not because it is still a wonder to see a person in flight, but because the character's victorious escape is shown by strongly visual action—a highly theatrical vision.

In Peter Nichols' *A Day in the Death of Joe Egg*, Sheila is the mother of Joe, a severely brain-damaged ten-year-old girl. As everyone else tries to convince Sheila to give up Joe to a managed-care facility, she desperately tries to convince us, the audience, that her hope is realistic. But we have seen Joe for ourselves, twisted and unresponsive in her wheelchair. Sheila finishes her plea with, "I believe where there's life, there's hope. Don't you?" And to theatricalize her hope, Nichols brings Sheila's imagined vision onstage.

> *The lights go off Sheila and come up brightly over the whole set, very strong, like a continuous lightning flash. Joe comes on skipping rope.*

> JOE *(Skipping)*: Mrs. D, Mrs. I, Mrs. F F I, Mrs. C, Mrs. U, Mrs. L
> T Y. *(She stops skipping.)* Ladies and Gentlemen, there will
> now be an intermission. Afterwards . . . we shall try to show
> you what happens when Sheila returns home with their
> mutual friends, Freddie and Pam. *(She bows then resumes
> skipping.)*

The soft light of Sheila's intimate monologue suddenly changes to blinding light; then the entrancing transformation of the crippled Joe into a charming, playful girl is visually stunning, heart-wrenching, and highly theatrical.

In John Guare's *Six Degrees of Separation*, the main characters—two straight-laced Manhattanites—quietly peek in on their charming, sleeping houseguest:

> *The stage is blindingly bright, Paul* [the houseguest] *sits up in bed. A
> naked guy stands up on the bed . . . the hustler naked but for a pair of
> white socks, comes into the room . . . stretches out on the sofa.*

Nudity in action has always been a theatrical spectacle. Unless our species evolves past hormones (a day I hope I don't live to see), it always will be theatrical since it stimulates body response. But static nudity, without movement, loses its theatricality and is reduced to centerfold titillation.

Spectacular sets and costumes can be theatrical—but only when used through action. Without actors, magnificent sets and costumes become stage sculptures. But when performers live on and move in or around them, they contribute powerful spectacle to theatre and are crucial elements of theatricality.

Movement and dance are elements of spectacle. Physical transformations such as television beauty makeovers, or a flower girl transformed into a duchess (*Pygmalion*) are spectacles. Fire, fog, and rain onstage is spectacle. Blood is spectacle. Any wide-eye–making, "oh wow!"–provoking, Industrial Light and Magic–ish event is spectacle.

Music and Rhythm

Music and rhythm have been part of theatre since its inception from ritual, dance, and epic poetry.

The natural world is highly rhythmic. (Counting the crickets' chirps will reveal outdoor temperature.) Irregular rhythms and tones such as the crackling of a fire or the babbling of a brook can be restful and reassuring, but when they're exaggerated (a thunderstorm or the howling of woodland animals), they become frightening. As noted earlier, the first sounds humans ever hear are the rhythms of their mother's heartbeat accelerating and decelerating in concert with the chemical reactions of emotional states.

Musical theatre capitalizes on the inherent theatricality of music to underscore dramatic action. In *Man of La Mancha*, the prostitute Aldonza struggles to revive Don Quixote:

> ALDONZA: You spoke of a dream. And about a Quest!
> QUIXOTE: Quest?
> ALDONZA: How you must fight and it doesn't matter whether you win or lose if only you follow the Quest!
> QUIXOTE: The words. Tell me the words!
> ALDONZA: (*"Sings."*)
> "To dream the impossible dream . . ."
> But they're your own words!
> "To fight the unbeatable foe . . ."
> Don't you remember?
> "To bear with unbearable sorrow . . ."
> You must remember!
> "To run where the brave dare not go—"
> QUIXOTE: (*Remembering, speaks then sings.*) "To right the unrightable wrong,"
> ALDONZA: Yes.
> QUIXOTE: "To love, pure and chaste from afar,"
> ALDONZA: Yes.
> QUIXOTE: "To try, when your arms are too weary,
> "To reach the unreachable star!"
> ALDONZA: (*Seizing his hand, kisses it.*) Thank you, my lord!

The scene, actually a dramatic dialogue, theatricalizes the despair, fantasy, and celebration through its use of music contrasted against the prose. Surefire tearjerker.

Terrence McNally's use of music is crucial to his plays' theatricality. *The Lisbon Traviata* allows the late Maria Callas' romantically tragic voice (and life) to theatricalize the love/pain of the main characters' relationships, a theatrical theme he explores more fully in *Master Class*. His *Frankie and Johnny in the Clair de Lune* uses the title composition to make tangible the magic of two people who find each other:

> *Debussy's "Clair de Lune" is heard again. Johnny sits, listening. He starts to cry he is so happy. He turns as Frankie comes out of the bathroom. She is brushing her teeth. Johnny sits next to her on the bed. They are both brushing their teeth and listening to the music. They continue to brush their teeth and listen to Debussy. The lights are fading. END OF THE PLAY.*

The prosaic routine of concurrent tooth-brushing juxtaposed against the heightened romance of Debussy's melodic strings theatricalizes the day-to-day with the magical romance that exist side by side in love.

The Emperor Jones, by Eugene O'Neill, theatricalizes through percussion the impending doom of the main character, who is ultimately murdered by his own fear. He journeys through the jungle for escape. A persistent drumbeat begins in scene 2 and builds throughout the play. As the characters hear and respond to it, an involuntary anxiety rises in audience response. Theatre.

> *He sits in a weary attitude, listening to the rhythmic beating of the tom-tom.*

As the play progresses and he travels deeper into the woods, his frantic dialogue is peppered with O'Neill's musical description:

> *The rate of the far-off tom-tom increases perceptibly as he does so.*
>
> *The beat of the far-off tom-tom is perceptibly louder and more rapid.*
>
> *The only sounds are a crashing in the underbrush as JONES leaps away in mad flight and the throbbing of the tom-tom still far distant, but increased in volume of sound and rapidity of beat.*
>
> *A low melancholy murmur rises increasing gradually by rhythmic*

degrees which seem to be directed and controlled by the throb of the tom-tom in the distance, to a long, tremulous wail of despair that reaches a certain pitch, unbearably acute, then falls by slow gradations of tone into silence and is taken up again.

Common in virtually every play but less obvious are the rhythms and music of language. Read—no, better, *listen*—to the opening of Peter Shaffer's *Amadeus*:

Darkness. Savage whispers fill the theatre. We can distinguish nothing at first from the snakelike hissing save the word Salieri! repeated here, there and everywhere around the theatre. Also, the barely distinguishable word Assassin! The whispers overlap and increase in volume, slashing the air with wicked intensity.

VENTICELLO 1: I don't believe it.
VENTICELLO 2: I don't believe it.
VENTICELLO 1: I don't believe it.
VENTICELLO 2: I don't believe it.
WHISPERERS: Salieri!
VENTICELLO 1: They say.
VENTICELLO 2: I hear.
VENTICELLO 1: I hear.
VENTICELLO 1: They say.
VENTICELLO 1 AND 2: I don't believe it!
WHISPERERS: Salieri!
VENTICELLO 1: The whole city is talking.
VENTICELLO 2: You hear it all over.
VENTICELLO 1: The cafés.
VENTICELLO 2: The Opera.
VENTICELLO 1: The Prater.
VENTICELLO 2: The gutter.
VENTICELLO 1: They say even Metternich repeats it.
VENTICELLO 2: They say even Beethoven, his old pupil.
VENTICELLO 1: But why now?
VENTICELLO 2: After so long?
VENTICELLO 1: Thirty-two years!
VENTICELLO 1 AND 2: I don't believe it!
WHISPERERS: Salieri!

Listen to how the rhythm of the language fuels the suspense and intrigue of the play. Just reading it builds nervous momentum much like the insistent tom-tom of *The Emperor Jones.*

Elizabethan playwrights such as Shakespeare used rhythm and poetry to unify the individual tempos of each audience member into the cadences of the play. Most commonly they used iambic pentameter (five unstressed/STRESSED beats per line) and rhymed couplets. This effective use of rhythm is used today in the disparate works of Sam Shepard, Tennessee Williams, Caryl Churchill, and David Hirson, among others.

Dramatic Foreshadowing

Anyone who has read *Moby Dick* in high school has undoubtedly been lectured on the literary foreshadowing of Ishmael walking through the whale's jawbone at the Spouter Inn. Now ditch it; *dramatic foreshadowing* has little to do with literature. Since we hold captive the audience's mind, heart, and bladders, theatre must constantly direct them on not only what they are seeing, but also on what they *will* see. When a scene you're watching is over, it's easy to shift attention unless you are already hooked into wanting to see more. This promise of "but wait 'til you see this!" is dramatic foreshadowing. It's relatively easy to spot; nearly anything written in the future tense of the play is likely to be dramatic foreshadowing. Anything that implies a potential action that will or could happen is another sign. Often a prologue does exactly that. Look at this example from Shakespeare's *Troilus and Cressida*.

> A prologue arm'd, but not in confidence
> Of author's pen or actor's voice, but suited
> In like conditions as our argument,
> To tell you, fair beholders, that our play
> Leaps over the vaunt and firstlings of those broils,
> Beginning in the middle; starting thence away
> To what may be digested in a play.
> Like or find fault, do as your pleasures are,
> Now good or bad, 'tis but the chance of war.

In the prologue's end, we are promised to bypass the rumblings of battle and begin deeply enmeshed in the height and theatricality of war.

Mark Medoff uses the same technique at the beginning of *Children of a Lesser God*. The play starts at the end of a violent argument in which James' wife fights in American Sign Language and storms off. Then James speaks to the audience:

JAMES: She went away from me. Or did I drive her away! I don't know. If I did, it was because . . . I seem to be having trouble stringing together a complete . . . I mean, a speech therapist shouldn't be having difficulty with the language. All right, start in the . . . Finish the sentence! Start in the beginning.

At the play's beginning, we are promised a dramatic fight, a relationship breakup, and the scenes that will make a successful speech therapist so unraveled that he can barely talk.

Look at the beginning of Peter Shaffer's *Equus*. In the opening monologue, we are similarly promised scenes that drive a reputed psychiatrist to question life. But before the doctor speaks, the opening image promises intriguing, albeit rather bizarre, theatre:

> *In a spotlight stands Alan Strang, a lean boy of seventeen. In front of him, the horse Nugget. Alan's pose represents a contour of great tenderness; his head is pressed against the shoulder of the horse, his hands stretching up to fondle its head. The horse in turn nuzzles his neck.*

Shaffer's use of the words *fondle*, *nuzzle*, and *great tenderness* indicate to the actor a, let's say, *more complex* relationship than Tim and Lassie. When we find out the same boy "blinded six horses with a metal spike," we are hooked. Totally involving, totally theatrical.

Samuel Beckett entitled one of his plays *Waiting for Godot*. The title alone implies a future event. The characters, Vladimir and Estragon, announce from the start that they are waiting for Godot's arrival. Yet, we look in the program and see that no character is named "Godot." We see Vladimir, Estragon, Pozzo, Lucky, and Boy. Does this mean that the dramatic foreshadowing is sabotaged? Remember that Beckett did not write a famous play; he wrote a play that became famous. The audience sees no Godot in the program, but we also hear Vladimir and Estragon only address each other by their nicknames, "Didi" and "Gogo." Will "Lucky" be a nickname for Godot? Maybe that is why the last character to appear is only listed as "Boy"? The audience becomes involved in the question by anticipating the answer, and this anticipation is a dramatic foreshadowing that holds you through the play.

Within a play, dramatic foreshadowing is expressed through scenes as the characters express warnings, hopes, fears, expectations, and dreams. If you've ever *begun* relating a story with "You'll never believe this!" (notice the future tense), you are creating dramatic foreshadowing. Here's an example from Edward Albee's *Who's Afraid of Virginia Woolf?*

> GEORGE: Just don't start in on the bit, that's all.
> MARTHA: The bit? The bit? What kind of language is that? What are you talking about?
> GEORGE: The bit. Just don't start in on the bit.
> MARTHA: You imitating one of your students, for God's sake? What are you trying to do? WHAT BIT?
> GEORGE: Just don't start in on the bit with the kid, that's all.
> MARTHA: What do you take me for?
> GEORGE: Much too much.
> MARTHA: Yeah? Well, I'll start in on the kid if I want to.
> GEORGE: Just leave the kid out of this.
> MARTHA: He's mine as much as he is yours. I'll talk about him if I want to.
> GEORGE: I'd advise against it, Martha.

While the audience waits for even the slightest mention of children, sons, or kids, the play continues. Another brilliant method of fore-shadowing is Albee's use of language and character. George and Martha are so brilliantly witty and boldly destructive that we never know what's going to happen or come out of their mouths next. This constant promise of surprise makes us hunger for more, just like watching a standup comic who keeps us laughing.

Elaine May's hysterically funny *Not Enough Rope* begins with similar foreshadowing, but since the tone is comedic, our delightful anticipation is peculiar in contrast to the highly morbid subject matter, and it hooks us right away:

But first . . . Does the last paragraph pique your curiosity and make you wonder about the play? It promises exposure to a play that is both funny and morbid. Your peripheral vision tells you there is a scene printed next. Is this paragraph the one you would stop at to pick up your dry cleaning before returning to the book? That's dramatic foreshadowing.

> EDITH: Hi there! I'm your neighbor across the hall. I was just wondering if I could borrow some rope.
> CLAUDE: Rope?
> EDITH: Yes, I'm awfully sorry to bother you but I've tried everybody else in the house and nobody seems to have any rope, and I just thought possibly you might have some. I

don't know why I thought that . . . (*She laughs.*) There really isn't very much reason for anyone to keep rope around is there?—unless they're planning to put up a clothesline—which there is hardly room for in these rooms or rather, place for in these rooms or room for in this place. (*She laughs inordinately.*) I hate to use the same word twice in a sentence. It's a thing with me.

CLAUDE (*After a moment*): I have twine.

EDITH: Oh. Would that be strong enough?

CLAUDE: Well, what did you want it for?

EDITH: I wanted to hang myself but I don't know if twine would hold me. (*She laughs again.*) I'm kind of a heavy package.

If that opening hooks you to see or read the rest of the play, then May's dramatic foreshadowing has succeeded.

Suspense

Suspense goes hand in hand with dramatic foreshadowing. Once something is promised, then the tension of anticipation can build to the point of creating suspense. This is so theatrical that an entire genre of theatre and film is based on it. If you've seen *Jaws* (the original), you remember how the eerie orchestration built suspense and had you digging your nails into someone's unfortunate arm.

Frederick Knott's *Wait Until Dark* is a brilliantly suspenseful play about a blind woman confronting murderers in her own home. From the start when three dangerous men are seen lurking around her basement apartment, to her husband's announcement that he must leave her alone that night, the suspense builds. By the climax, we are plummeted in the dark along with her as she smashes all the lightbulbs and we cannot see what happens. It's thrilling and, along with the spectacle of total blackness, highly theatrical.

In Marsha Norman's *'Night, Mother*, Jessie has told her mother at the beginning of the play her intention to commit suicide at ten o'clock. When ten arrives, her mother in denial finally grasps the scope and severity. Jessie attempts to say good-bye to her panicked mother:

JESSIE: Don't try to stop me, Mama, you can't do it.

MAMA (*Grabs her again, this time hard*): I can too! I'll stand in front of this hall and you can't get past me. (*They struggle.*) You'll have to knock me down to get away from me, Jessie.

I'm not about to let you . . . (*Mama struggles with Jessie at the door and in the struggle, Jessie gets away from her and:*)

JESSIE: (*Almost a whisper*) 'Night, Mother. (*Jessie vanishes into her bedroom and we hear the door lock just as Mama gets to it.*)

MAMA: (*Screams.*) Jessie! (*And pounds on the door.*) Jessie, you let me in there. Don't you do this, Jessie. I'm not going to stop screaming until you open this door, Jessie. Jessie! Jessie! What if I don't do any of the things you told me to do! I'll tell Cecil what a miserable man he was to make you feel the way he did and I'll give Ricky's watch to Dawson if I feel like it and the only way to make sure I do what you want is you come out here and make me, Jessie! (*Pounding again.*) Jessie! Stop this! I didn't know! I was here with you all the time. How could I know you were so alone? (*And Mama stops for a moment, breathless and frantic, putting her ear to the door and when she doesn't hear anything, stands back up straight again and screams once more.*) Jessie! Please!

(*And we hear the shot. And it sounds like an answer. It sounds like No.*)

The mounting rhythm of the dialogue, the dramatic foreshadowing of the suicide, and the spectacle of their violent struggle contribute to the scene's climactic theatricality. Then, look how long Norman leaves us alone with the mother before the shot. Our shoulders tense waiting for the startling crack of Jessie's pistol. The fact that we know that Jessie *will* kill herself heightens the suspense as we wait, knowing for certain what Mama does not. It makes a powerfully theatrical ending to an intimate drama.

Here are some other actively theatrical elements:

Grand entrances and exits: Mrs. Venable's elevator descent in Williams' *Suddenly Last Summer*; the Angel's parting promise into the heavens in Tony Kushner's *Millennium Approaches*; *Cyrano de Bergerac*'s rise out of the audience dressed impeccably with, "I am going to lose my temper!"

Contrasts and conflicts: Conflict is crucial to all drama and is obviously theatrical. Contrasts are comparisons or changes, such as the first and second acts of Neil Simon's *The Odd Couple*, in which Oscar's filthy, hurricane-hit apartment is transformed into a tidy, pristine home. Or the confrontation between the two contrasting characters of Claire Booth Luce's play, *The Women*, Mrs. Mary Haines—proper, dignified, and maternal—and Crystal Allen—tough, opportunistic, and hard as nails.

Death and **Sex**: Our strongest fears and greatest desires. Witnessing either one (rather than participating) almost always evokes interest and response.

Intensely emotional events: Juliet spotting Romeo (or Maria spotting Tony) and falling in love is theatrically involving. Mortimer discovering a dead body in his aunts' window seat (*Arsenic and Old Lace*), which also involves death. Othello's envious rage is theatrical. Jack Tanner's panic over being trapped by Ann in *Man and Superman* is theatrical.

Bizarre: People are continually impressed by the oddities in the world. (Perhaps it takes our minds off the weirdness in ourselves.) Giraudoux's *The Madwoman of Chaillot* is a pseudo-Countess impeccably dressed in the proper fashion of the 1880s but living in 1949. *The Elephant Man*, by Bernard Pomerance, is about a severely misshapen young man from a circus sideshow; sideshows are inherently theatrical. The bizarre world of Ionesco's *The Bald Soprano* is theatrical, as are the aberrant underworlds of Joe Orton's plays.

Humor: Since theatricality is any action that evokes audience response, then humor is a natural. The situations of situation comedies are generally trivial and untheatrical ("Lucy and Ethel build a barbecue"), but the humor keeps us involved.

Breaking the fourth wall: Oedipus, Viola, Salieri, and Sister Mary Ignacious all address the audience directly. Bill Irwin's *Largely New York*, a play without dialogue, uses audience members directly, as does Roberto Athayde's *Miss Marguerita's Way*. Interactive plays such as *Tamara* and *Tony 'n Tina's Wedding* involve the audience as unwitting cast members. Grabbing at the audience grabs the audience.

The elements of theatricality are innumerable and keep evolving as theatre artists continue to experiment with new technologies, concepts, and gimmicks. It is nearly impossible to have an effective play without at least some of these elements. If they're brilliant, it's theatricality. If they're cheap, it's theatrics. Regardless, they affect an audience, and theatre cannot communicate and succeed without theatricality. Capitalizing on the theatricality or theatrics of a script is not trashy; it's sensible.

- Theatre must communicate.
- Audiences must be focused in order for that communication to work.
- Techniques exist to grab and collectively hold that focus.

Theatricality is any technique that does just that. Look for the expressed or implied theatricality of the script and *use* it. If it's not there, *make* it. Plays don't work without it.

10   Stage Directions

When I was first learning the craft of playwriting, David Ball, one of the country's first resident dramaturges, told us, "Write your script as though you are sending a telegram and every word costs five dollars." I imagine he has upped that to ten bucks by now.

Fine playwrights use language as sparingly as poets. Since one of the requirements for theatre is to grab and keep an audience's attention, excess wordage slows down momentum and is assiduously avoided. There is not one word in a script's final publication that is not ultimately useful to an actor. The more important question is *how* it is to be used. Unfortunately, there has become a conventional practice that stage directions, especially descriptive adverbs, should be "crossed out" since they are impossible to play. True: They are unplayable. False: They are unusable.

One of the arguments is that great writers such as Shakespeare use little more than "enter, exeunt, they fight, etc." Yet it is foolish to compare Elizabethan playwriting to any era after it. To begin with, during that time plays were not published but were passed on directly much like traditional ballets were passed on before film or video recording technology was invented. During this passage of script to actor, the intention of the lines was conveyed by the playwright, whereas more modern writers would include stage directions.

Second, acting "technique" was scarcely developed until the nineteenth century, so subtleties of performance were included in the dialogue. Not only were the character's feelings stated directly, but so were the locale, mood, lighting, and thoughts written into the dialogue. Where Othello says, "I must weep, / But they are cruel tears. This sorrow's heavenly. . . ," there is no need for modifiers; the emotional content is written within the line. A more modern playwright might have written, "(Anguished) Oh god!" and allowed the actor to fill the moment with emotionally charged action rather than emotionally descriptive words. This is neither better nor worse, but a different style that has evolved in a different world.

Stage directions are one playwriting technique for eliminating unnecessary words. As playwrights' subjects evolved from gods to kings to aristocracy to the common man and woman, dialogue had to reflect a new kind of realism and naturalism. With this new writing style came newer acting techniques to enliven them. As acting became more subtle, rich, and truthful, emotionally descriptive dialogue seemed redundant and awkward. So rather than, "Behold, take this letter which I offer thee with heavy heart," the modern writer writes, "(Reluctantly offering letter) Here." Can you guarantee that you would have understood the meaning of the line if you had routinely crossed out all of the stage directions? Every bit of information that an author offers is potential fuel for creation. Eliminating it is wasteful and arrogant.

Another argument is that the subtle influence of stage directions even at first reading is too strong and interferes with the natural process of discovery. I like to give actors more credit than this. Everything in a script is subject to and reliant on actors' interpretation. Otherwise, few actors could effectively portray Stanley Kowalski, Hedda Gabler, Hamlet, or Lady Bracknell because the influence of past—even definitive—performances would be too strong. Certainly, these roles, for that reason, become more of a challenge to reinterpret uniquely, but actors with talent and technique are able to do so admirably. As long as actors understand that their job is to *translate all feelings and ideas into playable actions,* then the adverbs, stage directions, and actors' notes are only stepping stones or suggestions to be used, interpreted, or even discarded subject to the performers' judgment and creativity.

Again that magic "therefore" comes in. When Odets writes: "(Sheepishly) Jeez Edna, you get me sore sometimes!", ask yourself,

"I am saying this sheepishly—*therefore* what do I DO?" Without the stage direction, the line might be an attack, a threat, a surrender, or a complaint. Yet the playwright has specified a "quality" to the line. What does "sheepish" *do*? Perhaps he retreats, apologizes, or humbles himself. If the script is the heart of the production, then selective surgery of its contents is damaging.

This does not mean that stage directions are to be followed to the letter. They are strong suggestions from the playwright and, moreso, often reveal character traits. But some stage directions are less utile. For example, when Bernard Shaw was writing for publication, he hoped to make his descriptions as full and descriptive as though the production were being watched. He might even specify the angle of someone's nose or the exact pitch of their voice. This does not mean that you must have rhinoplasty and vocal stretching to play the part, but that you use your judgment in interpreting the *intention* of the description.

Blanche's entrance in scene 4 of *A Streetcar Named Desire* is described as having her knuckles pressed nervously to her lips while Stella lies serenely in bed. The scene follows Stanley's famous howl for "STELLA!" and Williams wants to convey the atmosphere after their passionate reunion. The actor or director may feel that "serenely lying in bed" is not the most active beginning of a scene with only one person onstage. The useful information is the stage direction's *intention* to show Stella's peace and satisfaction after a night of passion. *Must* she lie in bed? Not necessarily. Perhaps she is sweeping the mess off the floor, perhaps she is organizing beer bottles, perhaps she is checking her newly rounding stomach in the mirror. But most important is that *whatever* she chooses, it must be infused with the serenity and satiety conveyed in that direction. And we've all seen actors communicate their anxiety by pressing their knuckles so hard to their lips that one or all turn white. This choice might seem too dated or clichéd a choice for the artists involved. As long as the *intention* of the playwright's stage direction is followed, the specific choices are innumerable.

Given the accurate information by the playwright, an actor is responsible enough to make intelligent and inspired choices using all the crucial and elusive ingredients in the script. *But not all the "printed" information is accurate.*

One of the greatest challenges to script analysis is that the most affordable publications of scripts are not necessarily the actual script. Many of the plays popular to stock and amateur companies are published by these houses not as written, *but as performed.* In other words, rather than publishing the performance-neutral script, they publish the promptbook. (You've seen these: They are the typed, looseleaf-bound pages with all the scribblings, blockings, line cuts, and lighting cues for the last show you were in.)

Every production is performance-specific. The script is shaped, adjusted, and interpreted for the actors, audience, and location of the production. This tailored script becomes the promptbook—a blueprint of one specific interpretation. The advantage of publishing these books rather than the script is that less-skilled directors, or history teachers who adore theatre but have less training and love to run the drama club, will have a blueprint for a production that works—complete with prop lists, ground plans, and stage business.

The trouble is, it is impossible for the skilled actor or director to discern the author's intentions apart from the specific-production intentions. (I humbly plead for these houses to use a different typeface to differentiate!) No playwright is going to write, "Crosses D.R. to table." This is the job of the director, who may decide the table is going to be a filing cabinet and it be situated up left. Also, these modified editions may eliminate dialogue that is less comfortable to the stock or amateur audiences at whatever time the script was typeset. It is most important to buy accurate scripts, not "acting editions." For example, in Lillian Hellman's *The Children's Hour*, Karen confronts the ever-loyal Joe about lingering doubts he might have as to her guilt.

> KAREN: Joe, can we have a baby right away?
> JOE: *[Stage direction intentionally left out]* Yes, I guess so. Although we won't have much money now.
> KAREN: You used to want one right away. You always said that was the way you wanted it. There's some reason for your changing.

In one published version, after Karen asks about the baby, there is the stage direction "*(Laughs)*" before Joe responds. Therefore, Karen's reaction seems oversensitive when Joe is trying his best to move forward. But in a publication more accurate to the Hellman script, the stage direction reads "*(Vaguely)*." Then Karen's reaction becomes a keen perception; something *has* changed. Perhaps the production on which the prompt script is based wanted Joe to be the perfect supportive man. It seems more accurate that Hellman was trying to illustrate the infectious damage of rumors to the point that even Joe, a man of utmost integrity and loyalty, might doubt his fiancée.

The more advanced playwriting and acting become as our civilization evolves, the more subtle dialogue might become. Perhaps, with the influence of motion pictures, a style might eliminate dialogue altogether. In these plays, such as Bill Irwin's *Largely New York*, stage directions would be everything. Regardless, they are one of the very few *direct* connections the playwright has to the actor. Just like any connection between collaborating artists, they are neither commands nor ramblings. They are *recommendations* that reveal intention, higher ideas, and characterization. They are no more important than your creative interpretation and insights, yet no less important either. Don't "follow" them, don't *ignore* them: *use* them the same way you use every other element of this complex instruction manual we call a script.

111 Raisin Debtor

One sunny afternoon in the sixteenth century (then again, it could have been raining), an unprecedented block of flawless, white Carrara marble appeared on noisy wagons from the hillsides outside Florence. Its grandeur was so powerful that all the local sculptors were too intimidated to touch it—except one. Michelangelo stared deep into its whiteness and saw the great power of the human individual, which he carved into his masterpiece, the *David*. In that fourteen-foot statue, he froze the instant when young David makes the courageous decision to combat the enormous Goliath. With that one decision, diminutive David expands to heroic size and epic proportion. We stand at his base, his feet above eye level, and recognize that each of us can achieve superhuman dimension through powerful choice.

If that great sculpture were a NouveauStone coffee-table statue you'd have: naked guy with slingshot.

Bear with me, I'm making a point. Donatello sculpted the same subject, but instead he created a life-size bronze of David as an adolescent—mischievous, playful, and self-assured to the point of cockiness—a foreshadow of the giant he will become. Bernini sculpted David also from marble but chose the theatrical moment when David has reared his slingshot, thrown all his power into his arms, and is biting hard on his lower lip, in the instant before release. The difference in the appearance of Michelangelo's, Donatello's, or Bernini's *Davids* and *Naked Guy with Slingshot* is determined by *what point the artist is attempting to make*.

Although it is impossible for some ideas to be expressed in words (which is why we have so many great art works entitled *Untitled*), **all art exists for a reason**, a *raison d'être* as the French call it, or "raisin debtor" as some pronounce it. And this reason to exist is its *theme*, or *ruling idea*.

Theme is one of those words that people often confuse with *moral*:

> Mouse accidentally scampers into sleeping Lion's nose. Lion gets peeved. Mouse begs for his life—promises to help Lion one day when he needs it. Lion finds that concept so funny he frees Mouse. Years later, Lion gets trapped in hunters' net. Mouse finds him, chews through the ropes and sets him free.
>
> Moral: *No act of kindness, no matter how small, is ever wasted.*

Aesop wrote many of these fables with their accompanying morals. The fable is an uncomplex way of expressing one simple idea through story. Ah, if only life were expressible in just simple ideas.

Fables have morals, but plays have one or more theme(s) that cannot be expressed through one catchy saying such as "Love conquers all" or "Good triumphs over evil." A theme can be an overall idea, a concept, a human conflict, and often *a question*. But avoid distilling works of art into catchy sound bites. Would you like being summed up as a "dumb jock," "ditzy blonde," "boring nerd," "artsy type," or any other pigeonholed term in which the world likes to typecast us? The richness of a play's life should not be simplistically distilled anymore than a human being should be.

Michelangelo's themes in the *David* are power, heroism, and the beauty of human form. Alvin Ailey's dance "Revelations" includes ruling ideas of African and American valor, tradition, pain, and celebration. Themes in Beethoven's *Moonlight Sonata* might be mystery, constancy, and nocturnal passions. Picasso's black-and-white oil painting *Guernica* addresses the ruling ideas of war, inhuman cruelty, ugliness, and death. All great art has this thematic purpose even if they are simply about the immeasurable beauty and joy of life.

Unfortunately, when we hear the word *theme*, we hearken back to American Lit. 101 with its term paper about THE theme of *Moby Dick*, which the teacher then red-inks, "Wrong!" If you see a play and take from the theatre a new impression or inquiry you apply to your own life, how can it be wrong? And this is the most important part of drama's thematic raison d'être: After the final curtain falls and your own life resumes, something relevant stays with you beyond the theatre's aisles. It has not merely passed time; it has made a change. These are its themes.

The presence of ruling ideas that endure beyond the time limits of the piece make the difference between decoration and fine art; tunes and music; construction and architecture; or entertainment and theatre. Or existing and living.

Michelangelo made his abstract ideas tangible through stone, Beethoven through sound, Alvin Ailey through motion. Theatre does so through action. When abstract ideas are translated into observable action, theatrical themes emerge. Since all stage actions are performed by actors, and actors choose the strongest actions, then the actor who understands and interprets the strongest thematic ideas of the script has the greatest potential for making the most powerful choices for that play.

Themes of Time

For more than two thousand years, up until modern drama, plays' themes were classical in nature. In other words, a basic human philosophy existed that the world and its societies made a perfect machine with the gods as boss. Only when people screwed up did things go haywire. For the Greeks, that screwup was called *hubris*, which means a kind of "dark side" to human nature and, more specifically, is a kind of arrogant pride. When Oedipus swears that *he* will find the answer to Thebes' plague (presumptuous beast; plagues, floods, and famine are the gods' department), he goes blind, gets banished, and his brother-in-law takes over running the government. If he had a different destiny that allowed him to leave the gods to take care of it, Iocasta might have eventually gotten hit by a wagon, the plague would have ended, and Antigone would have grown up to make ol' Oeddy a granddad. The nature of classical ruling ideas suggest that only the gods (or who/whatever represents ultimate power) can properly run the world.

By the late 1800s, science and technology evolved to the point where humankind was thought to have been able to accomplish anything. Look at what was invented by inspired individuals during one fifty-year span beginning in 1853: lightbulbs, batteries, anesthesia, bicycles, color photography, telephones, phonographs, canned food, automobiles, X-rays, motion pictures, and, of course, the airplane. Suddenly the world didn't seem so much like a big machine with the gods (or equivalent) at the joystick. People could alter those wheels and gears. So theatre began to reflect this new perception. Rather than being held responsible for messing up a perfect world, the individual was now glorified for his or her unique vision that could repair an *imperfect* world. With Ibsen and Strindberg largely acknowledged as the first Modern playwrights, mathematic rhythms of poetry (the machines of language) were abandoned for realistic speech (the common language of the individual).

Plays can be divided between Classic and Modern drama with this kind of thinking. The themes of Classic drama are about the malaction of individuals. The themes of Modern drama are about the attempts of talented individuals to repair the imperfect world. Notice how these two enormous, generalized themes do not offer an answer or even suggest a specific statement; instead they propose subjects of discussion, contemplation, and imagination. Art does not preach; it presents.

But moreso, notice how important it is to know the *time* in which a play was written. When world power shifted away from the gods/church and toward commerce/trade, ultimate power became the government—kings rather than gods. When government shifted from royalty to republics, ultimate power became society. When societies accepted that "all men (and women) are created equal" and that even individuals from the poorest class could productively change the world, ultimate power was recognized as being within the individual.

Plays are not written for posterity; they are written for the contemporary audience for which they will be performed. *The Crucible* is about a small New England town in the throes of witch-hunting. It was first performed in 1953. But look at the time context: In 1950, Senator Joseph McCarthy advised the President that the government was riddled with communists. By 1951, there were fifteen million television sets in this country—ten times that of the year before. That year, Ethel and Julius Rosenberg were sentenced to death for espionage—and the conviction was made primarily on circumstantial evidence. The paranoid atmosphere that feared communist spies lurking everywhere built to the point that McCarthy had the whole country watching his "witch-hunt" trials on their new televisions by 1954. World War II had recently ended, and Americans had learned how the Nazis hunted down and exterminated races and cultures. This was the country's approaching climate that Arthur Miller observed and wrote about. How can you fully understand Arthur Miller's *The Crucible* without knowing the chronological context in which it was written? *Do you think the play is about witches in 1692?* For a modern audience, could it also be about the fear of sexually transmitted diseases?

Could an actor from future generations accurately play Tony Kushner's *Angels in America* without knowing what AIDS was (past tense intentional) and how it drastically changed the free sexuality of the previous thirty years that had begun with the invention of the birth control pill? Great ideas, from which great plays are made, are born from the eras in which they are created.

Theme and Playwright's Works

People (not characters—real folk like us) have themes. Whether we've devoted our lives to making music, fighting injustice, or figuring out what the meaning of life is, these are concepts that flavor every choice we make. Playwrights are people (although a number of producers might disagree with that), and often their body of work reflects recurrent themes.

Bernard Shaw directly expressed his strongest ruling idea in *Man and Superman*. In it, a young man panics at the prospect of marriage and spends the entire play escaping the woman destined to entrap him. During the third act's dream sequence, Shaw outlines "the life force principle." This principle suggests that the bipolar spirits of male and female must unify in order for our species ("man") to evolve into our greatest potential ("superman"). This is hardly a new idea, nor is it an old-fashioned one. The yin and yang of Eastern philosophy has shown this principle for centuries, and modern psychology/sociology explores the higher power we all achieve by embracing both the male and female within ourselves. Shaw's *Heartbreak House*, *Arms and the Man*, *Pygmalion*, and *Candida*—to name only a few—make this principle tangible through the action of these plays.

Tennessee Williams often wrote about the destructive conflict between our highest spirit and our basest animalism. Characters in *A Streetcar Named Desire*, *Cat on a Hot Tin Roof*, *Suddenly Last Summer*, and *Summer and Smoke* all try to battle high and low into coexistence, usually with tragic results. Often that high spirit is made active through the culture and dreams of the antebellum South, and that animalism is metaphorized through sexual desire and monetary greed.

Anton Chekhov contrasted illusion and reality, often allowing "real" events to happen offstage so that our contact with it is solely through the perception of his characters. They often escape the painful, compassionate, or productive truths by using self-deceit, trivial preoccupations, misdirected goals, and cold hearts. Almost a century before the "love children" of the 1960s asked, "Hey, like, what is reality, man?" Chekhov was posing the same questions through his plays.

Harold Pinter often explores themes of devastating loneliness. His dialogue only masks real communication, with its deepest truths *between* the lines. His characters reach out to each other but are from such diverse or individually perverse worlds that no real contact can be made.

Christopher Durang usually makes his simple but clear point that the whole world is insane. Therapists are insane. Nuns are insane. Government is insane. Parents, children, uncles, sisters, lovers—just trying to interact with another human being—is insane.

As for William Shakespeare . . . well, take every ruling idea there is to explore and you'll probably find it somewhere in those thirty-eight plays. Shakespeare left no human stone unturned.

Theme and the Playwright's Life

Frank Lloyd Wright is arguably the most important architect of the twentieth century. His houses—most famously the prairie-style Robie House in Chicago and FallingWater outside Pittsburgh—changed the scale, shape, and landscape of America. Although he created many large-scale public structures, his four hundred or so houses were his first love. With his massive Guggenheim Museum just completed in New York City, the project on his drawing board when he died was a small cottage house. If you research his life, you'll learn that his childhood family moved nearly everywhere between New England and Wisconsin; he lived in fourteen residences before he grew up. Does that illuminate why he obsessively created home after home, rooted in the landscape, with fireplaces and hearths as the central constant through all his stylistic evolutions?

Understanding the meaning of artwork by learning about the artist is a relatively new approach. But it is a double-edged sword. One edge shows it can be quite helpful. Take, for example, Eugene O'Neill, this country's first world-class playwright.

Almost always, a dominant force in O'Neill's plays is a tyrannical father figure. When O'Neill met his first wife, his father was so against the relationship that he shipped Eugene off to the Honduras. (O'Neill married his beloved right before setting sail, in spite of him.) His wife gave birth to a son but his father fiercely forbade Eugene to ever see them. Oddly enough, when Eugene returned from the Honduras, he conceded to join his father, a prominent stage actor, as manager of his theatrical touring company. Does this shed some light on the paternal characters in these plays?

The fact that O'Neill was born "in a trunk" and spent so much time growing up in and around theatres that produced largely melodramatic and unexceptional plays (just read anything American before O'Neill) might also suggest why his dialogue lacks the truthful ring of Thornton Wilder or Elmer Rice, who were contemporaries.

In 1922, he met an actress, Carlotta Monterey. By 1929 he married Carlotta (third's the charm); moved to Europe, where he was becoming widely accepted; returned to the U. S. for an honorary Yale doctorate (his college years at Princeton were a bomb); and created many estate homes throughout the country with his new wife. Perhaps for the first time he was able to let go of his traumatic past and even see some aspects of it with nostalgic satisfaction. Is this why, in 1933, he wrote his only comedy, Ah, Wilderness!, about a teenager and his family in 1906—which happens to be the same year O'Neill was that character's age?

This information can be helpful. If you examine O'Neill's life and conclude that Ah, Wilderness! is autobiographical, then you may also study another autobiographical play, Long Day's Journey

Into Night, which, in essence, has the same relationships and settings but with a severely contrasting perspective. Using this knowledge, you may play *Ah, Wilderness!*'s Richard as the mirror image of Edmond in *Long Day's Journal Into Night*, taking into account what you know about O'Neill's state of mind when he wrote it.

But the sword's doubled edge to this research can be as easily dangerous. What researching the author's life can do is make the actor a ten-cent therapist. Perhaps what really happened was, after living in Europe, O'Neill realized that there was another perspective on childhood. Perhaps, since O'Neill explored many writing forms, he wanted to take a crack at comedy. Perhaps his new wife was sick of his dark moods and insisted he lighten up. Perhaps it was a silly experiment that struck oil. It is impossible to be certain of another person's state of mind.

Unless we are lucky enough to meet the author directly, talk with him or her, and ask questions, the information we get is inevitably limited and certainly filtered through another writer writing about a writer. Playwrights are not characters that can be fully drawn through limited information—human beings are far more complex and contradictory than stage characters. How irritating is it for you when an acquaintance or teacher who knows a few details and observations makes confident conclusions about your motivations, personality, and problems? This is the danger of making confident conclusions about a play by knowing only *some* information about the human being who wrote it.

Nevertheless, gathering research about the artist can save time and suggest ideas you may not have considered as quickly. But use this information carefully, weighing it no more strongly than your own instincts and impressions of the play itself.

Learning about the play by examining the era and audience for which it was written is essential; reading the author's other works is extremely helpful; researching the writer's life can be quite useful; but learning about the play *from the play* is the most valuable.

Theme and the Play

Perhaps the latter half of the twentieth century will be summarized by Andy Warhol's famous prediction: "In the future, everyone will be famous for fifteen minutes." The alternate measure of success besides money is celebrity, and people grab any chance to become one of "The Beautiful People," even if doing so means exhibiting their most private shame on a talk show. It is no small wonder that the personal lives of artists have become as crucial as, if not more important than, the work itself.

But if you experience a work by an unknown creator—like the ancient Roman *Winged Victory*, the stunning madrigals of the Medieval period, a short story by someone you have never heard of, or even the Grand Canyon—you experience it on a purely personal level, uncluttered by the creator's history, motivations, or perceived temperament. You can develop a dialogue between your deepest self and an abstract creation. And that combination will allow the most profound and uniquely personal interpretations.

Six Degrees of Separation, by John Guare, is a play about a wealthy Manhattan couple, Ouisa and Flan, who bring into their home a young man with a bleeding stab wound from a mugger. Paul, the young man, is a friend of the couple's Harvard-educated children and also the son of Sidney Poitier. At least that's what he convinces them. The truth is that Paul is a stranger who had an affair with one of their children's friends. That friend taught Paul upper-class behavior as well as much personal information about many wealthy families. The plot reveals the serendipitous connection and deep impact between these diverse characters.

Let's search for clues that might suggest the play's largest ruling ideas. One of the first elements to consider in any script is its title. What does "six degrees of separation" mean here? The answer comes midway through the play.

> OUISA: I read somewhere that everybody on this planet is
> separated by only six other people. Six degrees of
> separation. . . . I find that (a) tremendously comforting that
> we're so close and (b) like Chinese water torture that we're so
> close. Because you have to find the right six people to make
> the connection. It's not just big names. It's anyone. A native in
> a rainforest. A Tierra del Fuegan. An Eskimo. I am bound to
> everyone on this planet by a trail of six people . . . How every
> person is a new door, opening up into other worlds. Six
> degrees of separation between me and everyone else on this
> planet. But to find the right six people.

This does not mean that the theme to this play is "we are all connected"—that's not a theme, it's a long-distance slogan. But it is a statement that helps illuminate a potential theme.

Two other helpful places to look are the first and last lines of the play: the introductory impression the author wants to make and the final thought he or she wants to leave you with.

In Guare's play, the opening image is stronger than the opening line:

> (A painting revolves slowly high over the stage. The painting is by Kandinsky. He has painted on both sides of the canvas in two different styles . . .)
>
> OUISA (with FLAN, speaking directly to audience): Tell them!

Immediately we are introduced to duality. Two very different parts of one whole. The actors speak directly to the audience: an immediate connection to us. And the last line:

> PAUL: The Kandinsky. It's painted on two sides. (. . . The painting begins its slow revolve.) The End

If we consider these three places alone—title, first line, last line—we begin to infer two thematic ideas. The first is about the marvelous and frightening concept that all humanity is connected no further than six links away. The second is that life experience is more complex than two-dimensional paintings.

Is this conclusive? Themes are rarely "conclusive"; they're too intimately reliant on the audience's personal interpretation. Nevertheless, your job as actor is to make thematic ideas concrete through your chosen actions. So continue your search by examining the expressed ideas and actions of the script.

First, look at the ideas directly expressed through dialogue. Guare shows us the perceived safe distance people maintain from those we consider to be "them."

> OUISA [speaking with a friend who makes his wealth in South Africa]: But we'd visit you and sit in your gorgeous house planning trips into the townships demanding to see the poorest of the poor. "Are you sure they're the worst off? I mean, we've come all this way. We don't want to see people just mildly victimized by apartheid. We demand shock." It doesn't seem right sitting on the East Side talking about revolution.

Later, Guare illustrates the unconscious recognition we all have of this intimate connection. Our search for it manifests itself in curiosity.

> PAUL: I was mugged. Out there. In Central Park. By the statue of
> that Alaskan husky. I was standing there trying to figure out
> why there is a statue of a dog who saved lives in the Yukon in
> Central Park and I was standing there trying to puzzle it out . . .

The couple, Ouisa and Flan, discover others who have been conned by the same boy. As they all share their similar stories, the play introduces a tangible question:

> OUISA: This kid bulldozing his way into our lives.
> LARKIN: We let him in our lives. I run a foundation. You're a
> dealer. You're a doctor. You'd think we'd be satisfied with our
> achievements.
> FLAN: Agatha Christie would ask, what do we all have in
> common?

The mystery escalates. Who was this boy, what brought him into "our" lives, and what do all the other victims of his con have in common? One thread they discover is that all their children attended the same boarding school. Ouisa and Flan's daughter, Tess, becomes involved. She suspects Trent, a former school friend, is the link. Tess seeks him out, and at the end of her investigation, says:

> TRENT: Look, we must keep in touch. We were friends for a brief
> bit in school. I mean we were really good friends.
> TESS: Won't you press charges?
> TRENT: Please.
> *(They go.)*

The last lines echo on Tess's concealed tape recorder.

> TESS: Won't you press charges?
> TRENT: Please.

The illusion of separateness is illustrated through Trent's fervent plea to reestablish contact. In truth, Trent *is* the connection; Paul has been linked to all these people through Trent's address book.

Guare has now shown us the two sides of the six degrees question: the obsessive curiosity of how all life is connected and the intense loneliness when we cannot recognize any connection. Seconds later, Ouisa gives the speech that defines the "six degrees" title and its "tremendously comforting" and "Chinese water torture" sides.

The play illustrates through action this concept. Paul is thrown out by Ouisa and Flan for bringing a hustler into their home the night they invite him to stay. Soon after, he meets a young midwestern couple, aspiring actors who live above a roller disco. His intensely intimate interaction with them incites the male to jump to his death. Another less-than-six-links connection surfaces at a dinner party:

> LARKIN: Kitty and I were at a roller disco two clients opened.
> KITTY: And it was Valentine's Day
> LARKIN: and we came out and we saw a body on the street.
> KITTY: My legs were still shaky from the roller skating which I have not done in I hate to tell you how many years and we knew the body had just landed there in that clump
> LARKIN: because the blood seeping out had not reached the gutter yet. . . . The boy had jumped from above.

The action of the play shows all the couples' children are spoiled and arrested in terminal adolescence. They attack their parents for their gullibility. The duality of life metaphorized in the double-sided Kandinsky is expressed again when Dr. Fine—another victim—calls his son Doug to verify Paul's identity.

> DOUG: The son of who? Dad, I never heard of him. Dad, as usual, you are a real cretin . . . Sometimes it is so obvious to me why Mom left. I am so embarrassed to know you. You gave the keys to a stranger who shows up at your office? Mother told me you beat her! Mom told me you were a rotten lover and drank so much your body smelled of cheap white wine.
> DR. FINE: There are two sides to every story—

The scene shifts to a flashback with the police. It then returns to the call:

> DOUG: A cretin! A creep! No wonder mother left you!
> DR. FINE: Two sides. Every story.

Again now, another connection:

> OUISA: —it's a black-tie auction—Sotheby's—
> FLAN: I know we'll get it.
> OUISA (*Noting the time*): Flan—
> FLAN: I know the Matisse will be mine—for a few hours. Then
> off to Tokyo. Or Saudi.

Suddenly, Paul calls Ouisa and Flan. The other side now, isolation:

> OUISA: Where have you been?
> PAUL: Traveling.
> OUISA: You're not in trouble? I mean, more trouble?
> PAUL: No, I only visited you. I didn't like the first people so
> much. They went out and just left me alone. I didn't like the
> doctor. He was too eager to please. And he left me alone. But
> you. You and your husband. We all stayed together.
> OUISA: What did you want from us?
> PAUL: Everlasting friendship.
> OUISA: No one has that.

Paul's call comes in the middle of a rebellious call from Tess announcing she is going to elope with a stranger and go to Afghanitan, and Ouisa cuts Tess off to speak with Paul. All the parents have a deeper connection to this stranger than they have with their own children.

Paul agrees to turn himself into the police when Ouisa promises to meet and escort him to the precinct, where she will demand civility and understanding. But the police precede the couple to the meeting place and they completely lose their tenuous connection to Paul. The Chinese water torture ensues. Guare reaches our hearts with poetry.

> OUISA: And we didn't know Paul's name.
> We called the precinct.
> Another precinct had made the arrest.
> Why? Were there other charges?
> We couldn't find out.
>
> We weren't family.
> We didn't know Paul's name.

We called the district attorney's office.
We weren't family.
We didn't know Paul's name.

I called the Criminal Courts.
I wasn't family.
I didn't know Paul's name.

The torturous frustration—the devastating loss of a deeply personal yet brittle link to another soul—is examined at play's end.

> OUISA: He did more for us in a few hours than our children ever did. He wanted to be your child. Don't let that go. He sat out in that park and said "that man is my father." He's in trouble and we don't know how to help him.
> FLAN: Help him? He could have killed me. And you.
> OUISA: You were attracted to him—
> FLAN: Cut me out of that pathology! You are on your own—
> OUISA: Attracted by youth and his talent and the embarrassing prospect of being in the movie version of *Cats* . . . And we turn him into an anecdote to dine out on. Or dine in on. But it was an experience. I will not turn him into an anecdote . . . How do we keep the experience?
> FLAN: That's why I love paintings.

Thematic ideas emerge clearly with this process without even beginning to relate it to the time it was written or the author's life and body of work. Examining the time, author's life, and work will certainly enhance your relationship with the script, but first allow yourself the chance for direct connection to the pure script without any prejudice.

So what is this play about? For me (and this is no more valid than what it may be for you because, once again, there is no "right" answer), it is about the double-sided ecstasy/agony of connection and loneliness. It is about how we distance ourselves for safety, and yearn for vulnerability and contact. Still, there are also numerous and strong questions about reality and illusion, phoniness and conjured truth, and other equally important facets that any individual might take away from the theatre as strongly as the themes I am most personally affected by.

It is that personal collaboration with an artwork that makes us want to see *Hamlet* dozens of times with dozens of *Hamlets*, or numerous *Death of a Salesman*s interpreted by numerous directors. And it's the personal collaboration of you as audience with an abstract life form that makes you want to see *The Cherry Orchard* one more time "now that I'm older and in a different place in life."

The actor becomes the soul of the character, and the ruling ideas become the soul of the play. Those two life forms are the deepest connections an audience has with dramatic artwork. After all, there is only one degree of separation between the life of the play and the life of you.

12   To Be...

> "Compared to everyday existence, dramatic theatre lures human beings from the poverty and triviality of humdrum experience to a vision of the infinite potentialities of life previously only vaguely felt."
> PAUL KURITZ, <u>THE MAKING OF THEATRE HISTORY</u>

By the time 2600 B.C. rolled around, Egypt was at its height of civilization. Their religion, like many Eastern religions, featured a strong belief in the afterlife and reincarnation. King Khufu began building the great pyramids of Giza to preserve his and his heirs' remains and possessions in order to make their journey to the next plane (and back again) safe and intact. It didn't work, by the way, since robbers broke in and stole everything, but it was a good try and we get one of the seven wonders of the ancient world to wonder at.

The entirety of the royal family's pyramids, guardian sphinxes, and temples was designed to protect the lifetimes of these people into the next world. Each individual pyramid, part of that entirety, was designed to transport one of those souls and their possessions. Each passageway and room in that pyramid was designed to confuse or kill looters, protect one set of possessions (which might include slaves or wives), or safeguard chariots and tools for the journey. And each brick was used to build one part of one wall to one room of one pyramid that was part of one great process that ensured immortality.

As we discussed in the last chapter, a playwright constructs a play with one or more themes or ruling ideas. Each character within the play's scenes has a *function* to illuminate those ideas. Each scene has conflicts those characters struggle against, which make that abstract idea visible. And each conflict has actions enacted by the character, all of which illuminate the ruling ideas of the entire play.

If we structure ancient Egypt like a play, its theme could be about ensuring immortality for the family. The characters might be: a Pharaoh, the Architect, Builders, and Slaves. The Pharaoh might have an overall desire to guarantee the pyramid's completion. The Architect's total focus might be to design a foolproof vault for his king. The Builder's overriding goal might be to control the construction slaves so that the blueprint's plans are carried out flawlessly. The Slaves' ruling purpose might be to perform the builder's commands well enough to remain alive.

These characters' overall desire/total focus/overriding goal/ruling purpose is what Stanislavsky called the *super-objective*. As the play has themes, characters have ruling objectives. As do people.

People have more than one super-objective since we are more complex than characters and we live in many chaotic "worlds" instead of the ordered focus of a play's. You may want to be a great actor, a parent of two children, blissfully in love, richer, thinner/bigger/gorgeous-er, or any number of goals. You act on each of these goals through various "scenes" of your life. Working on your script might help you become a great actor, dressing for your blind date might help you fall in love, or doing those reps might beef up those arms or tighten those abs, which shape you toward an ideal. A friend of mine has one life purpose of going to at least one baseball game in every stadium in the United States. Perhaps this is not the loftiest of super-objectives, but you can be certain that it affects every travel plan he makes. No business trip or vacation is arranged without a conscious effort to schedule it during baseball season in cities with unexplored stadiums.

At the beginning of this book, I suggested that you cross out "to be" and never use it except in one place. This is the place. The reason a super-objective can be a state of being is because you never play it. As in your life, you never play "being a great actor" or "being in love" or "being the father or mother of two children." You do play the thousands of actions that may achieve that goal.

Those thousands of actions are like the 2.3 million bricks that make up the Great Pyramid of Egypt. Hovering over the top of the pyramid is the theme of the play. First determine what you believe your character's function is within that idea. Are you the Builder? Pharoah? Architect? Next, choose the overall purpose of your character, your super-objective. It must function to elucidate the script's themes. If you were the Architect and you chose as a super-objective "to become rich and powerful," as many architects might, this would be irrelevant if the ruling idea was about ensuring immortality for the royal family. Therefore the actions of the play would all have to be whittled to fit the mold you arbitrarily chose.

After choosing a super-objective for the Architect, you could break it into two or three act objectives. For example,

Act I: Earn the Pharoah's commission

Act II: Design the greatest concept

Act III: Convey your vision to the Builder

Under each of these are scene objectives, which you begin to play directly.

Scene i: Beg an audience with the Pharoah

Scene ii: Prepare an impressive presentation

Scene iii: Inspire the Pharoah with your talent

All of these scene objectives are enacted in order to (Act I) earn the Pharoah's commission. Each of those scenes have smaller beats and actions until the script is broken down into the bottom row of bricks. And this bottom row serves as a linear time continuum, the moment-to-moment actions of the play.

The Pyramid of Objectives

On the next page is a *pyramid of objectives* using what is perhaps one of your super-objectives: to be a great actor. Let us assume that artists have a message to communicate to the world, and this message hopes to benefit humankind in some way. We will use this as the ruling idea for an actor/artist: to advance world civilization. The "play" could be constructed like Figure 12–1.

Under the theme of advancing world civilization, the simple

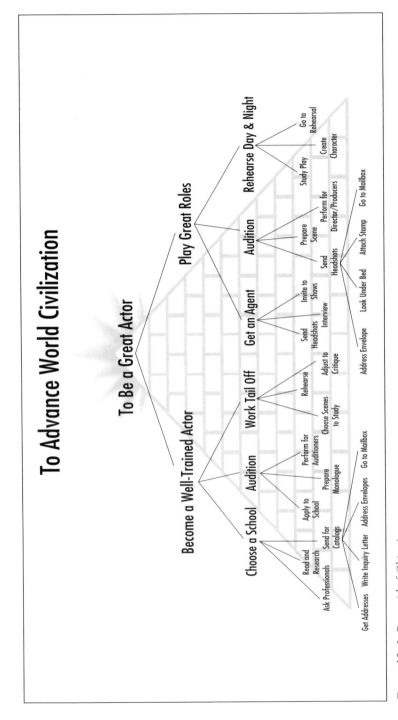

Figure 12–1 *Pyramid of Objectives*

action of addressing an envelope supports a great idea: You address an envelope, in order to send for catalogues, so that you can choose a school, that will help you become a well-trained artist, who becomes a great actor. In the second act of this play, you look under the bed, to find a stamp, to send your head shot, to audition for a part, to play a great role, that allows you to become a great actor. The bottom row of bricks represent each of those actions (too numerous to include in Figure 12–1), which enact a small scene, that builds a play, that supports the completion of a larger goal—the communication of a universal idea.

Yet unlike the people who constructed an Egyptian pyramid, the actor has one advantage: You don't have to worry about gravity. The Egyptians *had* to begin with the bottom row and the playwright usually gives you that to begin with—remember the script is a sequential listing of (bottom-row brick) actions. But you do not have to proceed in linear sequence. You can place a brick in the middle of the sky and fill in the ones below later. Sometimes the top brick, the super-objective, comes to you immediately. Other times it may not crystallize until the fifth week of performance. But as long as the pyramid is complete, your performance has a chance for immortality.

As an example, let's try to understand Willy Loman from Arthur Miller's *Death of a Salesman*. The play takes place shortly after World War II, when technology and young soldiers saved democracy from fascism. Masses of young men came home from the war wanting jobs, homes, and families. New electric appliances emulated streamlined rockets, and contemporary design replaced traditional and decorative arts. Inexpensive track housing and cheaply built apartments replaced old neighborhoods as young baby-booming parents-to-be devoured resources. For this example, we will choose themes of hero worship and the loss of the American dream.

Willy Loman is an ordinary salesman used up by the system. He has pursued the American dream he was raised to strive toward and is failing. He loyally worked thirty-six years for a company whose new young owner fires him. His grown sons, who once idolized him, abandon him to follow other dreams. Aged and exhausted, he tries to make sense of his life.

If we interpret that the play is about hero worship and the American dream, then what function does Willy Loman play in illuminating these themes? Willy is the common man who wants to be more. His skills and resources are insufficient yet he cannot accept his reality because the common man has become as expendable to America as World War II's frontline infantry. What does a man who knows he can be someone want when the world dismisses him as no one?

Creating a super-objective is one of the most personal and subjective character choices. It demands the most of your life experience, talent, and soul. So I ask myself what I would want in Willy Loman's shoes. First I focus on the ruling ideas in the script and then put myself in the Loman world. I see my dreams dissolving as I grow older yet further from my goals. I feel the increasing distance from my boys who once worshipped me. I watch my wife darning stockings because I cannot afford to buy her new ones, and my few possessions breaking down before I finish paying for them. What happened to my dream? Where is my shot at greatness? I want to strike gold for my family. I want to have fathered great sons. I want to be so revered at my job that every city hands me its key and when I die hundreds of salesmen and buyers travel miles for my funeral. I want to be Franklin Roosevelt. I want to be Dale Carnegie. I want to be John Wayne. *I want to be a hero!*

In Act I, I want back what I lost. With both sons home again and the house filled with the smell of shaving cream, I remember the days when Biff was surrounded by his idolizing brother and friends, and they all idolized me. I want that back. I want the company, whose owner put his arm around me pledging loyalty, to actualize the promises made across that desk. I want my shiny red Chevy, and the sun-filled garden, and my resourceful mind, and Boston, Hartford, Providence, and Albany to open their doors again. *I want it all back!*

In Act II, I must plan for the future. I cannot give up. I will demand a job that does not make me drive. I will inspire Biff to fight for himself and use his God-given talents to storm the world. I will even plant some carrots and beets and lettuce; they'll grow fine in a little light. And ultimately, I will give myself up so that my magnificent boy can begin his enterprises with twenty thousand dollars. *I must guarantee my family's future!*

Once I get back what I lost and guarantee its longevity, *I **will** be a hero. I know it!*

One of your challenges as an actor is to find a deep connection to your character. Deep connections are not made on the surface.

You don't fully *know* someone by eating with them, seeing movies, playing tennis, talking all night, having sex, raising a family, and growing old together. You fully know them by gathering *all* those experiences and synthesizing them into an overall picture. If you can predict a probable response to a new circumstance from that person, it cannot be because you've observed them in that circumstance before; it is because you can integrate all your experiences and intuitions into a human being *whose patterns make sense to you*. And if you want to *know* your character, you must understand them on a higher level than who they are, what they do, and what they want in individual scenes. You must synthesize what you know about them with what you know about life and yourself, and then create a unifying energy, a super-objective.

Could you perform Willy Loman—or any character—without a super-objective? Technically, yes. You never play it. No one sees it. No one even needs to ever hear about it. But the difference in acting *with* one and *without* one is like the difference between taking courses and aspiring for a degree: You can study each course with equal energy and commitment, but without aiming for that degree, the unifying goal for your hard work and the ultimate reason you complete each class is missing, and an overall aimlessness as well as a feeling of disconnectedness subtly thins your efforts. It's the difference between dating every week and committing to a relationship. Or the difference between writing sentences and composing a book. Or building a bunch of pyramids, and ensuring your people's immortality. Only with a unifying super-objective will your character become larger than life itself, universally affecting to the widest range of people, and potentially the performance of your lifetime.

13 The Greatest Shows on Earth

Theatre was born by playwright-performers; in the beginning they were the same person. Many of the finest playwrights of our civilization were also actors. Without plays, actors cannot learn their craft. Without rich roles, your growth proceeds at a snail's pace. Will you learn more from playing "Willy Loman" or "Wiley Lozenstein"? (Who's Wiley Lozenstein? Exactly.) You don't have to play these roles professionally; you can work scenes from them in a class. Or play them with friends in your living room. And you can learn a lot by simply reading these scripts in bed.

But skip the garbage. Potato chips are lots of fun, but you won't get any nutrition out of them. There's nothing wrong with M&Ms, but if they make up the bulk of your diet, you'll be nothing *but* bulk. We learn what our bodies need and nourish them accordingly. The more we discover about nutrition, the healthier we become, and therefore the richer our lives become. The majority of an actor's professional work could very well be commercial fluff. For every good play, there are at least twenty poor ones. For every good television script, there are at least eight hundred commercials. Odds are you'll be in one of those commercials before you're in one of those teleplays. There's nothing wrong with that—working as an actor in any capacity is noble—but while the business is feeding you

166

potato chips and M&Ms, make sure you nourish your artistic growth with Chekhov and Shakespeare. Or any great play.

This is where things get sticky. What exactly *is* a "great play," and who says so? Some are apparent: over hundreds of years, theatregoers agree that the works of Sophocles or Shakespeare or Molière are great works. (If you write something and two thousand years later people are still performing it, you've probably hit something.) But what about more recent plays? Or this season's plays? Success is not a measure of quality, and unrewarded genius in one's own lifetime is practically a cliché. Read over a historic list of Tony Award "best plays" or even Pulitzer Prize–winning plays and see what percentage you recognize. Like great presidents, the proof of a play's importance is highly subjective and can only be revealed over time. But the criteria for evaluation is consistent.

The following is a list of seven criteria for evaluating whether a script is a good one, a great one, or potato chips. *No* play is going to rise to all seven categories, and some great plays excel in only one, but a script that doesn't even satisfy a single element is most likely not an outstanding script and will have less to offer you than one that is.

1. The test of time: The script has lasting efficacy for more than its current generation. This is clearly the most foolproof method of judging a script's quality. Andy Warhol was right about the future's fifteen minutes of fame. In today's world where instant communication through airwaves and modem lines makes Hollywood prostitutes instant celebrities, fame and success are no longer measures. If you go to the library and look up news magazine covers of even one year ago, you'll be surprised to see how many of those faces you can't remember or can even recall the names.

But if a script is still relevant to your children, or grandchildren, or later centuries, then there is a power to it stronger than the individual or society that created it. Sophocles' *Antigone* and *Oedipus Rex* are still performed more than two thousand years later; are still retranslated, adapted, and interpreted; and still address an important truth about human nature and the still-unanswered question: What is life?

2. Universality: The script crosses specific cultures or nationalities. How many people today live in seventeenth-century, middle-class France? Yet Molière's *The Misanthrope*—about the hypocritical but necessary social graces of courtship and coexistence—enlightens and tickles twentieth-century Americans. *The Wedding Band* by Alice Childress is about a South Carolina black woman and a white man who are in love in 1918 when it is illegal for them to marry. But the play, which is performed all over the world, addresses prejudice and whether the individual should fight against or cooperate within the limits of an unjust society. A London high school girl forbidden to compete on the boys cricket team can relate to Childress' play as well as the two Nebraskan senior citizens who have fallen in love but know that marriage would drastically reduce their financial benefits.

3. Value: The script makes a statement of important social, political, psychological, or spiritual significance. Unfortunately, many well-written plays fall short because of the "so what?" factor. If you've ever listened to a long, detailed story from someone that finally forced you to interrupt with "what's the point?" then you have experienced the "so what?" factor. Drama grew in part from religious rituals, metaphors for great truths. When the play's fictional reality illuminates a perspective on life, then it is making an important statement. *King Lear* (among most of Shakespeare's plays) illuminates many life subjects, including responsibility, ego, family machinations, love, and honesty with oneself as well as with others. Sartre's *No Exit* confronts the truth of heaven and hell, and the questionable existence of any god. Ibsen's *An Enemy of the People* is about the individual conscience battling capitalism, and is perhaps the first play written about commercial pollution. The musical *On the Twentieth Century* makes the simple song-statement, "Life Is Like a Train," fast moving, exciting, fun, and adventurous.

4. Theatricality: The script is extraordinarily funny, moving, spectacular, and engaging. Theatre is an art form, and elements of its craft—if used ingeniously—can make a great play. Even though the social statements within Oscar Wilde's *The Importance of Being Earnest* fade in relevance, it is such a funny play that it will always be performed. *Cyrano de Bergerac* remains so heart-wrenching that, unless our species evolves past falling in love, it may always be cherished. The musical *Cats* has such spectacle that even without T. S. Eliot's poetry, people would have lined up to see it. Agatha Christie's *The Mousetrap* is so engaging that it has become the longest-running play in the history of London. A play can be great simply because it makes great "theatre."

5. Artistic significance: The script defines a period or style, or epitomizes a genre. Every art form has its genres. Dance has ballet, tap, jazz, folk, ballroom, and so on. As new civilizations continue to develop, so will new expressions. When theatre started, there was only tragedy and comedy. *Oedipus Rex* is the definitive tragedy. As art forms reflected evolutions of civilization, new styles developed. Ionesco's *The Bald Soprano* defines Absurdism. Congreve's *The Way of the World* defines Restoration Comedy. Rogers and Hammerstein's *Oklahoma!*, the first musical to have incorporated songs as integral plot points, defines American Musical Theatre.

6. Historical importance: The performance of the script has affected the course of human events. This is less likely today than it was centuries ago simply because the population has increased so vastly that theatre can reach proportionately fewer people than it used to. However, there are scripts that have spoken—and still do speak—so strongly that they ignite a fire in humanity. Pierre de Beaumarchais' plays (specifically *The Marriage of Figaro*) were influential in helping stir the French to revolution. In fact, its power was so frightening to the government that it was immediately banned. It was almost ten years before it was performed. Maxim Gorky's plays had a similar effect in Russia. Odets' *Waiting for Lefty* fanned the flames of labor unions' grievances. *Oedipus* and *Electra* served as models in Freudian psychology. The Mystery/Miracle/Passion plays of the Middle Ages influenced early Europeans' lives to follow properly the laws and values of Christianity.

7. Overall quality: It works. As you can probably tell from reading this book, every technical aspect of art has its intangible, immeasurable side. Some plays stand up for generations and eras simply because they "work." They are coherent, exciting, cohesive (all elements working in concert), clearly accessible to an audience on whatever level(s) they address, have characters that grow and are universally sympathetic, and/or use the tools of dramatic writing extremely well. Peter Shaffer's *Equus* works and Neil Simon's *The Odd Couple* works (whether this will destine them to be great plays remains to be seen). The vast majority of Shakespeare's plays all work. In 1818, the French philosopher Victor Cousin was the first to use the phrase "art for art's sake"; when theatre works, and works magnificently, it is **great** theatre for *theatre's sake*.

14! Playreader's List

For a short while, I did casting for a major off-Broadway theatre company whose season included Eugene O'Neill's *Desire Under the Elms*. At the time, there was a new crop of young film actors who achieved fame and heartthrob status relatively quickly, and the theatre's artistic director grabbed the opportunity to meet some of these new actors for some private, face-to-face heart-throbbing.

One of these actors (since then an Academy Award nominee) was on the artistic director's wish list. I called the actor in California to invite him to audition for the lead, "Eben." He agreed, thanking me for the opportunity, and expressed great enthusiasm for legit-imizing his new film career with serious New York stage work. But my respect for his good film work and artistic commitment dropped considerably when the first of his many questions began with, "So, what kind of play is this—comedy, drama?"

Now, it is impossible for a performer to know the entire body of dramatic writing; in two and a half millennia, that's a ****load of reading. There's also nothing wrong with not knowing all of the im-portant plays—which can take a lifetime to read or see. However, a serious actor should at the very least *recognize* which plays are con-sidered important. You should know the difference between *Titus*

Andronicus and *Tillie's Tumor*. Only a fraction of actors have read all thirty-eight of Shakespeare's plays, but every actor should be able to distinguish all of their titles. If a director mentions she is doing *Coriolanus* next season, or even *Merchant* . . . , the serious actor *knows* which two plays she is talking about.

It's a disadvantage that so much of American culture is based on passive viewing—whether it's the movie screen, picture tube, or monitor I stare at now while writing this book. There's an active involvement in reading. And the process of reading words without images creates a vacuum that is filled by the imagination, or "the mind's eye," as Shakespeare put it. The actor who reads constantly exercises that imagination. The actor who reads knows how to express ideas through words. The actor who reads understands articulate playwright language, and the actor who reads is far more desirable to the directors and writers who ultimately choose the cast.

The worst thing you can do when working on a role is to begin by *seeing* someone else play it. The concrete impact of seeing a role brought to life overshadows the subtlety of imagination. How easy is it to forget about Marlon Brando when you read *A Streetcar Named Desire*? But a talented actor who has never seen Brando's performance (unlikely as that may be) finds it easier to discover a fresh perspective than one who has. Rely on your perception and imagination. In other words: *Read, dammit!*

In the following section, you will find a list of plays that I believe actors should know. It is a *purely subjective* list and serves only as a general outline for your own evolving priorities. In the years that I have passed this list on to students, it has changed many times. New authors become significant, old authors seem frivolous, and the list changes with almost every theatre season.

Also, observe that they are primarily pieces from Western civilization. There are centuries of Asian, Mid-Eastern, South American, and African plays that were not included here simply because producing theatres in this country choose not to find the commercial potential for them—although, happily, this is beginning to change—and this book was written primarily for American and European actors. Nevertheless, you must recognize that the few plays listed here only scratch the surface of Western drama, and even less of world theatre.

As Americans, and moreso as members of the approaching

bimillennium, we must acknowledge that our species is a mix of rich, diverse cultures, each with its own unique expression and perspective on life. Human existence is what we all have in common, and the Eurocentrism of contemporary theatre is a disservice to all audiences. Only you can change that by expanding the repertoire and by learning as much as possible about the rich dramatic library Western civilization already has.

The plays are listed by overall category, and then by significance. More important than reading them in the order I've listed is reading them according to what *excites* you the most. The list can take a lifetime to "complete" and should *not* be rushed. And there is no reason to go in any specific sequence: Some people like reading all important works by a specific playwright; others prefer to read contrasting works of a period; others enjoy hopping along the time continuum with inspired haphazardness. ALL of these methods are perfectly valid as long as it remains an informative pleasure, and *never* an arduous chore.

Greek Tragedy and Comedy

Aeschylus: *The Oresteia (Agamemnon, Libation Bearers, Eumenides), Prometheus Bound*

Sophocles: *Oedipus Rex; Antigone; Electra*

Euripides: *Medea; The Trojan Women; The Bachae*

Aristophanes: *Lysistrata; Frogs*

Medieval

Familiarize yourself with the cycle (miracle) plays, including *Everyman* and *The Second Shephard's Play*.

Renaissance

William Shakespeare: *Hamlet; Macbeth; King Lear; Othello; A Midsummer Night's Dream; Romeo and Juliet; The Taming of the Shrew; Henry IV; Richard III; The Merchant of Venice; Twelfth Night; Antony and Cleopatra*

Ben Jonson: *Volpone; The Alchemist*

Christopher Marlowe: *Doctor Faustus; Edward II*

John Webster: *The Duchess of Malfi*

Early French, Restoration, and Eighteenth Century

Molière: *Tartuffe; The Misanthrope; The School for Wives; The Learned Ladies; Le Bourgois Gentilhomme*

Edmund Rostand: *Cyrano de Bergerac* (written in 1897, but in eighteenth-century style)

Richard Brinsley Sheridan: *The Rivals; The School for Scandal*

Oliver Goldsmith: *She Stoops to Conquer*

William Congreve: *The Way of the World*

Early Realism

Anton Chekhov: *The Seagull; The Three Sisters; The Cherry Orchard; Uncle Vanya; The Marriage Proposal* (one-act); *The Boor* (one-act)

Ivan Turgenev: *A Month in the Country*

Henrik Ibsen: *A Doll's House; Hedda Gabler; Ghosts; The Wild Duck; An Enemy of the People*

August Strindberg: *The Father; Miss Julie; Ghost Sonata; The Stronger* (one-act); *The Dance of Death*

Luigi Pirandello: *Six Characters in Search of an Author*

Bernard Shaw: *Man and Superman; Saint Joan; Pygmalion; Heartbreak House; Mrs. Warren's Profession; Major Barbara; Caesar and Cleopatra; Arms and the Man*

Oscar Wilde: *The Importance of Being Earnest; Lady Windermere's Fan*

Modern European Drama

Bertolt Brecht: *Mother Courage; The Caucasian Chalk Circle; The Jewish Wife* (one-act); *The Good Woman of Setzuan; The Threepenny Opera*

Samuel Beckett: *Waiting for Godot*; *Endgame*

Georg Buchner: *Woyzeck*

Garcia Lorca: *Blood Wedding*; *The House of Bernarda Alba*

Jean Genet: *The Maids*; *The Balcony*

Jean-Paul Sartre: *No Exit*

Arthur Schniztler: *Reigen* (better known as *La Ronde*)

Jean Giraudoux: *The Madwoman of Chaillot*; *Tiger at the Gates*

Eugene Ionesco: *The Bald Soprano*; *Rhinoceros*

Jean Anouilh: *Antigone*; *The Waltz of the Toreadors*

Modern British Drama

John Osborne: *Look Back in Anger*; *The Entertainer*

John Millington Synge: *The Playboy of the Westem World*; *Riders to the Sea*

Sean O'Casey: *Juno and the Paycock*

Harold Pinter: *The Birthday Party*; *The Caretaker*; *The Homecoming*; *Betrayal*

Noel Coward: *Private Lives*; *Blithe Spirit*; *Hay Fever*

Joe Orton: *Loot*; *Entertaining Mr. Sloane*

Tom Stoppard: *Rosencrantz and Guildenstern Are Dead*; *Arcadia*

Caryl Churchill: *Cloud Nine*; *Top Girls*

Terence Rattigan: *Separate Tables*

Athol Fugard (South African): *The Blood Knot*; *Master Harold and the Boys*

Christopher Hampton: *The Philanthropist*

Brian Friel: *Dancing at Lughnasa*

Modern American Drama

Eugene O'Neill: *Desire Under the Elms*; *Ah, Wilderness!*; *Long Day's Journey Into Night*; *The Iceman Cometh*

Tennessee Williams: *The Glass Menagerie; A Streetcar Named Desire; Cat on a Hot Tin Roof; Night of the Iguana*

Arthur Miller: *Death of a Salesman; All My Sons; The Crucible; A View from the Bridge*

Clifford Odets: *Waiting for Lefty; Awake and Sing!; Golden Boy*

William Inge: *Bus Stop; The Dark at the Top of the Stairs; Picnic; Come Back, Little Sheba*

Thornton Wilder: *Our Town; The Skin of Our Teeth*

Elmer Rice: *The Adding Machine; Street Scene*

Edward Albee: *The Zoo Story* (one-act); *Who's Afraid of Virginia Woolf?; A Delicate Balance; Three Tall Women*

Lillian Hellman: *The Children's Hour; The Little Foxes*

Sam Shepard: *Buried Child; Curse of the Starving Class; True West; Fool for Love*

Lorraine Hansberry: *A Raisin in the Sun*

Maxwell Anderson: *Mary of Scotland*

William Gibson: *The Miracle Worker*

Baraka (LeRoi Jones): *The Dutchman*

Neil Simon: *Barefoot in the Park; The Odd Couple; Brighton Beach Memoirs, Biloxi Blues, Broadway Bound* (trilogy)

David Mamet: *American Buffalo; Glengarry Glen Ross; Speed-the-Plow*

John Guare: *House of Blue Leaves; Six Degrees of Separation*

Alice Childress: *The Wedding Band*

Paul Zindel: *The Effect of Gamma Rays on Man-in-the-Moon Marigolds*

August Wilson: *Ma Rainey's Black Bottom; Fences; The Piano Lesson*

Lanford Wilson: *The Rimers of Eldritch; Burn This*

Tony Kushner: *Angels in America*

otes

The specific versions or translations I cite of plays are listed here by chapter.

Introduction

Pinter, Harold. 1978. *Betrayal*. New York: Grove Press.

Chapter 1

Churchill, Caryl. 1982. *Top Girls*. London: Methuen Drama.

Euripides. [431 B.C.] 1974. *Medea*. Translated by Paul Roche. New York: W. W. Norton & Company.

Fornes, Maria Irene. 1978. *Fefu and Her Friends*. Baltimore: The Johns Hopkins University Press.

Goldman, William. 1966. *The Lion in Winter*. New York: Vintage/Random House.

Hansbury, Lorraine. 1959. *A Raisin in the Sun*. New York: Signet.

Hellman, Lillian. [1934] 1979. *The Children's Hour*. New York: Vintage/Random House.

Marlowe, Christopher. [1588] 1932. *Doctor Faustus*. New York: The Modern Library.

Molière. 1961. *Tartuffe*. Translated by Richard Wilbur. New York: Harcourt Brace & Company.

Shaw, Bernard. [1916] 1966. *Pygmalion*. Baltimore: Penguin Books.

Stoppard, Tom. 1968. *The Real Inspector Hound*. New York: Grove Press.

Waxberg, Charles. 1996. *An Alternate Recipe*. Unpublished at press.

Williams, Tennessee. 1947. *A Streetcar Named Desire*. London: New Directions Publishing Corp.

Chapter 2

Shanley, John Patrick. 1984. *Danny and the Deep Blue Sea*. New York: Applause Books.

Chapter 4

Odets, Clifford. 1935. *Waiting for Lefty*. New York: Grove Press.

Chapter 5

Albee, Edward. 1962. *Who's Afraid of Virginia Woolf?* New York: Scribner/Simon & Schuster.

Odets, Clifford. 1935. *Waiting for Lefty*. New York: Grove Press.

Chapter 6

Gibson, William. 1960. *The Miracle Worker*. New York: Scribner/Simon & Schuster.

Chapter 7

Ibsen, Henrik. 1952. *Hedda Gabler*. Translated by Eva Le Gallienne. New York: New York University Press.

Chapter 8

Euripides. [431 B.C.] 1974. *Medea*. Translated by Paul Roche. New York: W. W. Norton & Company.

Mamet, David. 1992. *Oleanna*. New York: Vintage/Random House.

Miller, Arthur. 1949. *Death of a Salesman*. New York: Penguin Books.

Molière. 1961. *Tartuffe*. Translated by Richard Wilbur. New York: Harcourt Brace & Company.

Nichols, Peter. 1967. *A Day in the Death of Joe Egg*. London: Rochelle Stevens & Company.

Norman, Marsha. 1978. *Getting Out*. New York: Dramatists Play Service.

Shaffer, Peter. 1974. *Equus*. New York: Scribner/Simon & Schuster.

Shaw, Bernard. 1903 [1960]. *Man and Superman*. Baltimore: Penguin Books.

Wilde, Oscar. [1895] 1965. *The Importance of Being Earnest*. New York: Avon Books.

Williams, Tennessee. 1947. *A Streetcar Named Desire*. London: New Directions Publishing Corp.

Wycherly, William. [1672] 1965. *The Country Wife*. Edited by Thomas J. Fujumura. Lincoln, NE: University of Nebraska Press.

Chapter 9

Albee, Edward. 1962. *Who's Afraid of Virginia Woolf?* New York: Scribner/Simon & Schuster.

Guare, John. 1990. *Six Degrees of Separation*. New York: Vintage/Random House.

May, Elaine. 1964. *Not Enough Rope*. New York: Samuel French, Inc.

McNally, Terrence. 1988. *Frankie and Johnny in the Claire de Lune*. New York: Dramatists Play Service.

Medoff, Mark. 1980. *Children of a Lesser God*. Clifton, NJ: James T. White & Company.

Norman, Marsha. 1983. *'Night, Mother*. New York: Farrar, Straus & Giroux.

O'Neill, Eugene. [1920] 1959. *The Emperor Jones*. New York: Vintage/Random House.

Shaffer, Peter. 1974. *Equus*. New York: Scribner/Simon & Schuster.

Shaffer, Peter. 1980. *Amadeus*. New York: HarperCollins.

Chapter 10

Hellman, Lillian. [1934] 1979. *The Children's Hour.* New York: Vintage/Random House.

Chapter 11

Guare, John. 1990. *Six Degrees of Separation.* New York: Vintage/Random House.